From Kabul
with Love

From Kabul
with Love

Letters from a 21st Century Pioneer

Compiled by Dr. Faith Goldberg

Castle

From Kabul with Love
Published by Castle Publishing Ltd
PO Box 68-800
Newton, Auckland
New Zealand
www.castlepublishing.co.nz

© 2010 Faith Goldberg

ISBN 978-0-9582822-5-3

Typesetting:
Andrew Killick

Cover design:
Mishi Goldberg

This book is dedicated to Mum, who through her love transforms every house into a home.

With gratitude to all who helped to compile this book; Ruth Salinger for her wise counsel and for the final proof reading; Judy, Zellah, Betsy and other members of our writing group, and Naomi and her husband Pieter for all their practical help and encouragement.

After these things I looked, and behold, a great multitude which no one could count, from every nation and all tribes and peoples and tongues, standing before the throne and before the Lamb, clothed in white robes, and palm branches were in their hands; and they cry out with a loud voice, saying, "Salvation to our God who sits on the throne, and to the Lamb."
Revelation 7:9&10

Foreword

My Dad was a pharmaceutical chemist in New Zealand, with a long and strong involvement in foreign missions. Faith has recorded the private letters which passed between father and son over many years. We never thought of publishing them, but enjoyed a close and loving relationship which was only broken by the death of my father in 1976.

Is it still possible to enjoy such a relationship? Read, see and learn for yourself! I left for Central Asia from New Zealand in 1953, and have rarely been back to my home country, but have enjoyed a life of freedom and joy, serving in Central Asia.

Howard, March 2009.

Contents

Prologue – "Beginnings"

Story time with Dad was reserved for holidays. Life as an eye doctor in Afghanistan was demanding and most evenings there wasn't time for stories. Once a year our family escaped from land-locked Afghanistan to the coast of the Indian Ocean in neighboring Pakistan. We stayed in a two roomed beach holiday house, an hour's taxi ride from Karachi. After supper the family would gather around the table again and Dad would read us ancient tales of Troy and Greece and stories of heroic missionaries of the late nineteenth century, such as Hudson Taylor, or Mildred Cable travelling with her companions across the wild Mongolian Gobi desert, or George Hunter dying alone in Kansu, a distant province of China.

"Who would take George Hunter's place and reach Central Asia with the gospel?" Dad's eyes filled with tears and we three girls squirmed uncomfortably with his unusual display of emotion. Fumes from the kerosene lamp flickered in the center of the table and a musty salt tang permeated the beach house as Dad continued:

"I was fifteen when I said to God, 'I will go.' I knelt by my bed one night and said, 'I will go for You to Central Asia.' I woke up my older brother, Blyth, who slept in the same room, to let him know that I was going to Central Asia. He was half asleep and not amused."

I was nine when Dad related this call to us girls, and I had little idea of the geographical extent of Central Asia or that, living in Afghanistan, I was in a country considered to be part of Central Asia. It wasn't until I did some research for this book I realized that Central Asia covered an enormous expanse from the Caspian Sea in the West to Central China in the East. In the mid '50s, when Dad dedicated his life to God and Central Asia, most of these countries were inaccessible, isolated from the rest of the world by Soviet domination or strict Islamic rule. How my parents crossed these apparently impenetrable borders, one by one, unfolds in this story.

The second time I saw my Dad cry was on Naomi's fourteenth birthday, two days after Christmas. I had always felt sorry for my older sister who often had joint Christmas and birthday presents, but I pitied her even more this day because Granddad had died on her birthday. We received an early morning phone call from New Zealand; Granddad Stan had gone home to be with his Lord. At breakfast Dad played us a cassette recording that his father had made for us some months earlier during our last visit to New Zealand. We knew at the time he was dying from cancer, and I had wept on the return flight from Auckland to Teheran as I remembered the lean figure at the end of the departure hall waving farewell. Now as I listened to his last message I couldn't share my father's grief; Granddad Stan seemed so distant and detached from me.

Not long after my Granddad's death my parents decided to return from missionary service and establish the family in the garden of England, Kent. We packed our belongings in the Range Rover, and traveled overland to England. At the age of twelve, the door had closed on my Central Asian world … and it remained shut until 9/11.

A month after we watched two planes smash into the World Trade Center, our eleven inch TV screen showed scenes of rugged mountains and turquoise skies, deep gorges and rushing rivers, winding roads and hairpin bends – the rugged landscape of Afghanistan. Fierce men with rifles squatted with a bowl of tea in one hand; women veiled from head to toe in drab *burkas* trailed children whose eyes were clustered with flies. This world had once been mine. As I watched the news coverage of US fighter planes criss-crossing wide expanses of desert and flying above dragon-scale mountain peaks, I wanted to open the door that had closed on my Central Asian world, to open that unread chapter of my life again.

In their retirement my parents have adopted the nomadic way of life that historically characterized dwellers along the Silk Road. They winter in Eridge, Kent, migrate to Kabul after the snows there have melted, after some months they move on to Mongolia for the warmer late spring period and then mid-summer they fly to Israel to stay with our family for a few weeks. On one of these visits I supplied my Dad with a pocket dictaphone and half a dozen cassettes asking him to tell his life's story. Well practiced in dictating letters to secretaries, he effortlessly filled the cassettes. On a later visit Dad brought two carton boxes containing piles of letters, mainly in aerogramme form.

"These should help you out with your book" he said, "Information straight from the horse's mouth."

As I read through letters I discovered that Dad had corresponded with his father, Stan, every week for over twenty two years. A pharmacist by profession, Stan had meticulously kept, numbered and filed according to date, each one of Dad's letters. In a more haphazard fashion my Dad had also saved most of Granddad's letters. There were over one thousand letters, spanning the time Dad left New Zealand by boat for Pakistan in 1954, to when we settled in England twenty two years later.

As I read the dialogue between my Dad and Granddad, the shadowy lean figure waving farewell leaped into three dimensions and a moving partnership emerged, not only of father and son but the key role my Granddad played in my Dad's life as a mentor and home-front support raiser. After my parent's marriage in 1960 my Mum joined the letter duo, adopting Granddad in place of her father who died when she was twelve. As becomes evident in some of the letters, Mum held the strings that kept Dad's visionary kites firmly anchored to the ground, allowing them to soar high.

In my patchwork of letters, I have not removed the darker colors. I believe the drab and murky highlight the beautiful contrast of a real God working in and through the lives of an ordinary family to accomplish His extraordinary purposes.

In the mid '50s most of the countries of Central Asia were inaccessible – locked in behind the "Iron Curtain".

Chapter 1
The Conviction

*Howard's departure by ship for Pakistan
Auckland wharves, December 1953.*

In Karachi
Sunday 17th Jan 1954

Dear Mum & Dad

You've no idea what a thrill it is to me to be able to write these words "In Karachi" at the top. When we stepped off the "Dara" onto Pakistani soil, it seemed to me to be a decisive time in my life.

In some ways it marked the beginning of a new era; the end of one period of training, in which you both have been the major influences for good, to a new phase of preparation. So far you have never been too far away, Dad, to prevent me making foolish mistakes. The fact that now you are a long way away was borne home to me when I read your letter, which Mr. Williamson gave me. You had only just received my letter from Freemantle, which is in the remote past for me now.

The fact is a path lies ahead, that under the hand of God, must largely be decided by myself. However, although you cannot join in the fray of my life in the active way you have before, it is comforting to know your eager interest, as encouraging spectators of "the race".

Mr. Williamson was down at the boat to meet us about 7:30 am. We had breakfast and were through customs by 9:00 am. Guess what? I only had to pay about $2:00 customs. All the medical kit got through. They did not even ask if I had any, and they made out the customs forms. So, my conscience is void of offence. They did not even open our cases and were eager to help us get through. What a contrast to the rapacious rascals in Bombay, they squeezed the last possible anna out of us. Immediately my heart warmed to the Pakistani people.

Well I must close, love to you all and Bloafer.

Howard

*Farewell party at the wharf – Howard's older brother
Blyth (Bloafer) and Mother.*

32 Mumtazabad
Multan, W. Pakistan
Feb. 4th 1954

Dear Dad

I'm just waiting for tea, so will start to pen these few lines.

We are now immersed in Urdu. In fact at the moment it is above our heads. I'm really sweating to keep up the pace. The pronunciation doesn't worry me so much, but in writing I'm way behind. Colin is way ahead of me in the writing, but way behind me in pronunciation.

I think we are placed in an exceedingly good position to learn the language. Robbie is tremendously keen to push us ahead and spends hours drilling us in the different aspects. He is inclined to lose his patience if things do not go well. Then we have a local language teacher (munshee) two hours a day. If we don't get the language in record time, it will not be the fault of our teachers. Actually, after awhile your brain gets so soaked that it cannot take any more in.

Incidentally, it is grand not to have an encumbrance such as a wife. I can see what a great hold up a wife would be at this stage of things.

After tea …we had a really good tea; rich meaty soup, half a tin of NZ corn beef with a casserole of potatoes and cabbage, followed by custard made from powder with dried NZ apples in it.

Yesterday, I must confess I had a big burst of homesickness. I don't feel so bad now, but it certainly hurt for awhile. I also felt strongly drawn by two legitimate things, the desire to study medicine and the desire to study more theology. I do not know what to think of these things, Father dear. What do you think? Should I consider them at all, or should I forget about them all together?

Much love
Howard

32 Mumtazabad
Multan, W.Pakistan
10th Feb. 1954

Dearest Dad

Colin is not keeping in the best of health at the moment. Please don't tell his mother, let him tell her himself. The trouble is his stomach, not so much diarrhoea, although he's suffered several bouts of that.

Two Rough Old Mates, Colin and Howard, Multan 1954.

Since Jean has been at Shikapur, the food has not been very good, as can be expected when three bachelors are let loose.

February 21ˢᵗ – After a hard week of language study we went on a trip to Bahawalpur. This was the best trip yet. It had all the excitement of venturing into the unknown, and plenty of surprises when we got there.

Bahawalpur is ruled by a native prince and no missionary has ever lived there. It was rumored that they would not allow bible portions to be sold there. This made us all the keener to go.

We arose at 4:00am Saturday morning with the objective of boarding the Quetta express, which goes through Multan at 5:00am. to Bahawalpur. It was cold, and as we got ready to go it started to rain. This did not dampen our enthusiasm. It was also pitch black and Colin was the only one with a lamp. Before we had gone half a mile the gentle trickle had increased to a downpour. My trousers were soaked; however we pressed on to the station, and rushed to buy our tickets (third class), only to find the train was running an hour late. I promptly squatted by the fire of a tea seller on the station and dried my trousers.

The journey took three hours to do the 80 miles, but it didn't seem long, there was so much of interest. Arriving in Bahawlpur at 8:30am we had some breakfast in a city café. You would have died if you had seen all the dirt and flies, but we made sure that all we ate had been cooked. After that we got straight into selling books in the bazaar. An hour and a half later we had sold all the books that we had brought.

Much love
Howard

127 Karangahape Road
Auckland, N.Z.
Feb. 16th 1954

My dear Son

Many thanks for yours of the 4th with its news of your doings and yourselves. I wish I could sit down quietly and write when I feel like it, but Selwyn is on holiday now from the shop. I don't seem to get a moment from morn till night, and also have had a run of meetings, hence the jerky letters.

I'm so glad to know that your things traveled so well. As you are having electricity installed you will not find much use for the Coleman lamp or kerosene stove, but you may be glad of them later when 'out back'.

I've been thinking, son, about what you mentioned regarding your desire to study medicine and theology, but have no clear word on the matter. Naturally, the first and most important thing is to be in the will of God. So far as one can see, your present task is to become proficient in language and to make a start in this term to do what you can of evangelistic work. Any attempt to turn aside would seem to indicate that one has gone forward prematurely and not sure of His will. During this term you may learn definitely whether your primary task is direct evangelism or some other form of service.

However, if you are feeling attracted in either of the above directions, don't be in a hurry to dismiss the thought. Let it simmer quietly in your mind, pray about it, and above all do with all your might the work that the Lord has given you to do now, without distraction.

You are continually in my thoughts, how much more in His.

Much love from
Dad

Howard's father, Stan, outside of his Chemist shop,
Karangahape Road, Auckland.

32 Mumtazabad
Multan, W. Pakistan
25th Feb 1954

Dear Dad

It is Thursday evening, Robbie and Jean are still away, due to return on Saturday. So, I will take the chance of this quiet evening to have this little talk with you on paper.

Now I plunge into a rather difficult subject, my fellow workers. I would appreciate it if you would keep it under your hat. Colin and I see each other 24 hours of the day, both having sharp angular characters we tend to rub each other. We both compete and try to show we are better than the other man. This could be alleviated somewhat by commonsense measures, for instance if we had separate rooms, then particularly aggravating characteristics would be kept to your own four walls.

The same applies to Robbie, we have been thrust together far too much when Jean was away.

However, it is early to say that this is going to settle into a permanent state of affairs. After all, there is the great energy of the Holy Spirit striving within each of our breasts, to bring us to love one another in reality and there is "the Prayer of Faith". In these I put my trust.

Colin has had several frank discussions with me and in that direction the air has been cleared a great deal, and we have reached a better understanding.

Well, I think I have said enough about a very unpleasant subject.

Much love
Howard

32 Mumtazabad
Multan
18th March 1954

Dear Dad

The hot weather has really come. The past days have beaten anything that NZ could ever produce. We have shut the doors and windows and just sat inside and sweated. Fortunately, at night the heat lets up and makes it easy to sleep.

We are now thinking of escaping this heat and going up to the Murree hills earlier than we expected. As soon as we finish the 25 Urdu lessons that we have to cover, we are planning to up anchor, and away to Murree. At our present rate of progress that should be in some four weeks time.

March 29th – I think it must have been your "Prayer of Faith" that won the day in the difficulty I had with Robbie. Now it is possible to look back at a distance with the main part of the battle over. I really think it was a most decided attack of the Evil One. It never entered my head, in my wildest dreams, that I would be a cause of friction to Robbie. Perhaps if I had been expecting trouble, I would have been somewhat prepared in spirit for the attack- but I wasn't. The only thought I had was that we would work with Robbie along the lines of "Calvary Road". So you can imagine how perturbed I felt when friction began to appear.

We are keeping in fair health. Just after last weekend I had a slight return of diarrhoea and Colin has had a bad dose, the worst since he has been here.

Hope you are well, receiving times of refreshing from the Lord.

Much love
Howard

Learning Urdu with a munshee,
Murree language school.

127 Karangahape Road
Auckland, New Zealand
April 24th 1954

Dear Son

What a treat it must be to enjoy the change at Murree. The cool mountain air will soon be ever so much colder.

Regarding the motor cycle – I'm sorry if I barked a bit, son – many of my letters are dashed off against time, and I'm still a father telling his son what to do! Really, down at the center, I've committed you to Him and know that although you may make mistakes, He will see you through. Sometimes I get worked up and write my natural reactions first. Then, when I have prayed about it, I realize that you are in His care.

Folk here won't be shocked about the motor cycle if you do not advertise the purchase, and the less said about the price the better.

Glad to hear of the doings at Dingley Dell. Don't be worried over the higher cost of living in Murree – language school is essential and one can quite expect the Lord to meet the need as it arises.

There has been a set-back for us with the housing proposal in Milton Road. The builder saw Mother on Monday night with a proposal of what we had suggested. But his price was so far above what he had originally named, that I don't feel very interested. I will leave Mother and the builder to argue it out between them, as to a revision of the plan or the price.

I think that's all just now, son – except that I'm pleased that Colin's appetite is returning and hope his board is not raised in consequence.

Much love from
Dad

Stan and Esther Harper, 5 Wembley Rd, Auckland.

Dingley Dell
Kashmir Point,
Murree, Rawalpindi
Wed. 21ˢᵗ April 1954

Dear Dad

Today is one of those difficult sort of days, when faraway Auckland has power to charm and life here seems inexpressibly dull. Perhaps today more than ever before has been brought home to me the force of those words "Lord, suffer me first to go home and bury my father".

There, too, comes thoughts of other training that I would like to be doing, and at this time these things have power to tempt. It is good, I suppose, that all days are not cloudless. In a way it is selfish to be so cast down, especially when you think of the storms others are going through and the extremely difficult lot of so many of the brethren here in Pakistan. One wonders at such times whether it is right to have such ambitions as studying medicine, whether perhaps they are only self-inspired ambitions. I think it is the most difficult thing to know, whether one's motives for doing things are selfish or not. It even seems possible to live a most self-sacrificing life from selfish motives.

Friday- it has continued to be wet and cold, and as I look out of the window it is raining again and it promises to be a stormy night.

Yesterday afternoon, during a very pleasant walk in the bush, the Lord faced me with the question of medicine. It seemed He definitely wanted to confront me with the decision of whether I should go right through with it and take the necessary training, or whether to forget all about it. After an hour or two of very peaceful thought over the matter, I quietly told Him that I was ready to pay the price and go through the medical training. I knelt on the bush track and dedicated to Him any skill He might give to my hands and any mental knowledge that He might give.

There is the important question, of what those who sent me out will think about this new step that the Lord has called me to. I can only trust that those who really sent me out, those who know the Lord, will be prepared to see the Lord's hand in it. I realize that there will probably be those who do not approve at the beginning, and whose approval and prayers will only be won as the years show the reality of this step. But I trust that there will be some anyways, who will be able to share this "Call" with me, through the difficult, yet I believe, victorious years ahead of training.

I have not felt free to mention it to Colin as yet, nor to anyone else, but I'm prepared to do so any time.

I was most interested to hear about the new house proposition. Mum's heart was set on that brick house all along. I hope that she will be satisfied now that action is in sight. Make sure and give yourself a decent sort of study.

Much love
Howard

127 Karangahape Road
Auckland, New Zealand
May 5ᵗʰ 1954

My dear Son

Yours of April 21ˢᵗ deserves a longer answer than this will take, but I must be brief and try to cover the necessary points as I may.

Regarding your discussion with the Lord about a medical future, I know you want only to do His will, and if this is His guidance He will make it plain. You have taken the first step, in being willing to yield all to Him. Whatever comment I may make, you must not think I am trying to guide you – you must let HIM do that.

First let me comment that I am so thankful you have decided not to tell Colin this. Adjustment to the new life is difficult enough for both of you, but I think it must be costing him heavily and it would be cruel to face him just now with the prospect of having to face the future without your company. I hope you will not mention your decision to anyone else, until the Lord is opening your way in that direction.

You realize, I think, that his commendation and yours was pretty well a joint affair. All felt that though they would not care to send either of you alone, it would be alright if you went together. A breach between you would be interpreted as a victory of the enemy in separating brethren, or possibly that your going out was premature. I have already said that it seems likely to me that it may be necessary to stay together through this first term of service, do some gospel work, thus establishing the confidence of those at home.

As you know, the folk who give to missions have one interest, the preaching of the gospel and the winning of souls for Christ. Few would divert their giving from this, to support a medical student.

You will see, I think, the wisdom of saying nothing before the time comes, so that the Lord can order your way aright and lead others, too, into fellowship about the matter.

I will enquire about water sterilizing tablets.

Much love from
Dad

Dingly Dell
Kashmir Point,
Murree, Rawalpindi
20th August 1954

Dear Dad

It is with a considerably lightened heart that I am able to write to you tonight. All this week, since recovering from the dysentery, I have been under a deep fit of depression and in fact homesickness. But through a talk with Colin the weight has lifted. What has made me glad is that I may see your face again sooner than I expected.

After some thought, I mentioned to him my desire to undertake medical training, and the developments so far. He was not surprised and his suggestions were very helpful. He suggested taking the course in NZ, as he thought it may not be necessary to have matriculation in order to enter Varsity. Perhaps you could enquire into this?

Well I must say it was a tremendous weight off my mind to talk with Colin. Unconsciously, I felt I had been holding out on him. I do not say that I fully fall in with his advice, but I must say that it seems to me very worth listening to.

Today the draft from the assembly for the motorbike arrived! It has taken over twenty days to arrive here by airmail. The envelope looked really battered, so we can give thanks to the Lord that it got here. It came just in time, as we plan to begin looking for a motorbike sidecar when we are in Lahore, and that is only three weeks from now.

One pleasant feature of Murree is that there appears to be two springs. When we arrived all the wild flowers were blooming, and now all the flowers are out again. It is very beautiful.

Much love as ever
Howard

Howard with a beard, Kashmir Point, Murree.

127 Karangahape Road
Auckland, New Zealand
August 30th 1954

My dear Son

Yours of August 20th arrived yesterday, August 30th, so it is quite up to date.

Glad you were recovering from the dysentery, and hope that you will acquire some sort of immunity, or else cultivate a regime that will safeguard you from infection. Squire's companion to the B.P says, "Two tablespoonfuls of vinegar to a quart of water as a soak for raw vegetables destroy the bacillus of typhoid. Raw vegetables thus soaked for an hour and a quarter are rendered harmless." Ask some of the older hands what their experience has been.

In view of your chat with Colin, and what you have just written,

I'm glad that I thought through the issue on Sunday. I'm sending what I wrote then, without alteration, for you to think through.

"It would seem odd to me if your course of preparation is to last until you are 34 years of age. If the Lord needs a doctor, I imagine He would be more economical in the expenditure of time, though I may be wrong.

Entrance to NZ medical school is highly competitive, as in Britain. To enroll as a medical student one must pass the medical intermediate exam, with Stage 1 in three subjects. To be able to sit this exam, one needs matriculation. Last year, out of the forty sitting the exam, 18 passed. Of these, only two were sitting the exam for the first time."

All of which sounds as if I'm a bit of a wet blanket!

The Kodachromes of Delhi Gate and Robbie preaching in the street are nice and clear.

Much love to you from
Dad

Robbie preaching in the street, outside a factory in Multan.

Rawalpindi Bus Station
Friday 18th Sept. 1954

Dear Father

Just before I left Taxila Hospital this morning, they handed me your last two letters. So, coming up to Rawalpindi in the train I had something to read and think about.

This is surely the queerest position that I have ever typed a letter to you. It is 1 pm and burning hot. I am sitting alone in a bus just outside the 'Pindi bus station. It was supposed to leave at 1 pm, but no one is in sight yet.

I began to recover from the fever a little on Thursday. In my opinion, it was the natural healing forces asserting themselves, rather than the malarial and other drugs that were given. I confess I still do not feel 100%.

I'm going up to Murree. As you will remember, I left the bike up there. I also received a letter from Colin and some much needed cash. He said that things in Lahore were very crowded and advised me to stay out of Lahore as long as possible.

I haven't had time to think about the letters you wrote. I do think, however, that about the education you tend to be pessimistic. Of course I was a failure at Grammar School, since I didn't study I could never be anything else. My first efforts at real study were at BTI (Bible Training Institute). Without becoming a work-slave there, I was able to do quite comfortably in the exams. This was followed by the most strenuous pace of study in my life, at Wycliffe. Despite the fact that at this time my mind was plagued with love questions, I was able to come out with B's and A's for the course. Then, although there was no exam in the missionary medical course, I felt I got the utmost benefit from it. Last, there is the language exam which we have passed with five months of study – a thing that has never been done before. While I do not claim brilliance, I think in the past years I have proved, to myself anyway, that I can absorb subjects which may or may not be interesting.

Having looked at the matriculation syllabus I realize my lack in Physics and Chemistry, but can see very little Mathematics. The only place that the Mathematics comes in is in Physics equations, and Colin reassures me that it is a simple type of algebra that is involved.

So far this letter has been written on the bus, during the frequent stops. I hope that you do not feel that I am not taking notice of your advice, but am hoping that my recent record, (which the Lord is responsible for), will be considered rather than the past, over which the Lord had only a very slight control.

Well, I must close now, as the bus is about to move off again.

Much love, Howard

B.O.A.C House
(British Overseas Airway
Cooperation)
Karachi
5th October 1954

Dear Dad

Just on the eve of departure. I promised in the cable sent today that I would write. So much has happened since I last wrote, it is hard to start.

I guess you are wondering just how I feel. The answer is, tired. The rush of getting documents, settling affairs and saying farewell, as well as the travel and cholera immunizations, has just about knocked the stuffing out of me. There is a sense of peace though. I do feel that although I have made some mistakes, in the major decision of going – I have made no mistake. Once the decision was taken, all things began to "work together", until this moment of stepping on the plane.

Please excuse me if I'm not very lucid, but it is 12:30pm. We have just arrived at the airport. There was a telegram waiting for me from Lahore with the content of two cables, one from the elders at Wiremu Street and one from the Edinburgh Medical Missionary Society. Edinburgh advises: "Wait for my letter", and the elders: "Elders disapprove". It is now impossible to turn back and I must go through these red lights.

I realize now, that if I did make a mistake, it is that I did not take the brethren at home into confidence before this. I did take the brethren here into confidence, and they were of the opinion that if I really felt called to medical work, I should go now.

I hope I can make it clearer to you all when I get time to sit down and think clearly about it, although I realize that only the future years will show whether this has been of God or not.

Well, there is the call to board the plane. Your $50 arrived just before I left Lahore. Thank you, I should be giving to you, it seems all wrong.

Love, Howard

127 Karangahape Rd
Auckland New Zealand
October 9th 1954

Dearest Son

Now that I've put paper in the machine, I don't know where to begin, unless it is to say that, whatever happens, I love you just the same.

You know that through all these months I have had no rest or light as to your proposal to exchange the ministry of the word, for the ministry of medicine, and have urged you to lean entirely on the Lord and get guidance from Him. Now that you are clear in your own mind, who am I to disagree?

You will find, I expect, that a good many will react strongly to the suddenness of your action. So far as I can see, son, your guidance seems to have been a strong inward conviction, such as mother gets when she wants to buy a house. No doubt you have thought of some of the things that are involved, but some have obviously missed your notice.

At any rate, it is too late for me to say much about the many things I've thought of – I've lived through all the difficulties of the next few years (in my mind), until there is little I have not thought of.

At the present moment the total amount you have in the A.N.Z Bank and the Auckland Savings Bank is $245. The A.N.Z Bank is able to remit a little over $100 of this amount any time you want it. For further remittances I'll need to apply to the Reserve Bank for permission. Will you please think about your plans for the future along this line, and tell me how you propose to finance yourself, and what amount you budget for a years' expense?

Naturally I'm wondering where you are this Sunday; perhaps in

London. Alone in London? But I cling to this, the Lord will never leave or forsake.

Mother is rejoicing that you have escaped the "commos" and the dysentery. She thinks it's a great adventure. Yesterday, she sold Martin Ave. for just a little above what she paid.

Am longing to hear from you, but know your letter will have reached me before this reaches you.

Much love from
Dad

127 Karagahape Rd
Auckland New Zealand
October 12th 1954

My dear Son

I had hoped there would be a letter from you today, Tuesday, as we've not had one since yours from Lahore, just after talking through things with Dennis Clarke. Maybe there will be one tomorrow.

Earlier today I cabled you, as we do not know yet whether you have arrived in Edinburgh, nor how you are. I made the cable reply paid, as I guess you will not have a surplus of cash. Unless I hear to the contrary from you, my idea is to cable $100 to an Edinburgh bank.

With the timidity – and perhaps cowardice- of increasing age, I am ashamed to think how I have dreaded the hardship of the course you have chosen, as though the Lord were a hard and austere master. These mornings in prayer He has been precious in calming my fears and showing me that whatever you face, He will be with you and will also give you the rich compensations known only to those who are walking with Him.

So I could go on writing, but must stop in time for the mail and hope this soon reaches you.

There are many things I want to say, but must do so a bit at the time.

Much love from
Dad

.

Chapter 2
The Confirmation

Student life – Howard skiing in Austria, 1954.

Medical Missionary
Society
31 Bedford Place
London W.C.1
21ˢᵗ Oct 1954

Dearest Dad

It is nearly a week since I wrote, and I hope that I don't have to live through another week like this. It has been a very worrying sort of week.

I received your cable while in Edinburgh, last Wednesday. I did not answer for a day or two because I was not certain of the address there. When I did answer I still gave the wrong address, as now I have finished off back in London and not Edinburgh.

I must say your cable was an encouragement to me. In Edinburgh there was a good deal to contend with. First, I was living in the YMCA, which was terribly dismal and depressing. The food was all of the pie and chip variety and most of the other occupants seemed drinking types that you would associate with a homeless shelter rather than a YMCA. The head of the Medical Mission was most unhelpful and "couldn't care less". Then, the medical school authorities gave little hope of getting in. So, on Friday, I decided it was time to go to Dublin.

On the basis of my talks in Dublin I decided to go to London and there try for the GCE (General Certificate of Education). If I can get the exams in the right subjects, I can apply to any University in the British Isles.

The main value of the trip to Scotland and Ireland was to give me first-hand knowledge of the universities and their peculiar problems of entrance.

I arrived here in London on Monday, and have since been prospecting around for a reasonable place to study. Dr. Johnson got me lodging at the Medical Missionary Society (MMA), situated near the British Museum and London University. I could not be more central, a really good set up – single rooms, good food, not too many chores. Just around the corner is a coaching school. Money is getting very short.

Well, it will be wonderful to settle down again to study, after a month of continually moving around and of mental stress and strain.

Much love
Howard

Looking down Bedford Place road, London.

31 Bedford Place
London W.C.1
26th Oct. 1954

Dearest Father

Yesterday I received the three letters from you, written to Edinburgh. For the last few days my mind has been so occupied with study that these letters still came as a shock to me. I realized that my move would stir up a storm at home, but now I see that I have paid nothing, and you have paid everything. Somehow it does not matter to me very much that the waves and billows of trouble roll over my head, as that is my affair. If they are for my own foolishness, they are well able to be endured. But it seems a very hard thing to me, that you should bear the brunt of my troubles.

Wednesday – I have just finished a hard day at the coaching school, Borlands. I had my first tutorial hour today and spent the whole time going over some basic algebra. I found it very difficult. In fact, at times it left me with a blank feeling of hopelessness. Still, I felt that way quite often when I began to study Urdu, and after a time it went.

The letters back from the eighteen or so hospitals that I have written to, asking for entry for next year, have not been very encouraging. Only one hospital actually sent the application papers back and said "go ahead and apply". The others said, "Sorry, full up for next year. Apply for 1956!"

You ask regarding finance. I fear this year will be rather expensive. I cannot get off with much less than £8-5-0* a week. I have found a place where I can get a lunch for about 2/-.** But the basic

---

* Eight pounds, five shillings and zero pennies – worth about £145 in today's money
** Two shillings – worth £1.74

costs of tuition and board are hard to cut down. I expect if the Lord did not send enough money to work at the studies full time, I could take a job somewhere and go to school at night.

Friday morning – I really must get this letter away. I have been looking back over the events of the past few weeks, and I am inclined to agree with Colin, that one cannot reasonably explain them at the moment. There are too many forces involved that will have to wait until a few years have added calmness, before they can reasonably be interpreted. The thing of course for me to be sure of is that this move was the result of a HOLY calling, and not just my own desire. As far as I can humanly see, it was the will of God and not my own. So far, although things have been difficult, yet it is obvious that the hand of the Lord has been in control.

Well, I think I have covered after a fashion all that I have to say.

As ever, much love
Howard

31 Bedford Place
London, W.C.1
10th Nov. 1954

Dear Dad

How the days are flying away! In no time at all it will be Christmas. It has been an interesting week, full of work and meeting new and interesting folk.

My Urdu marks arrived from Pakistan. I got 64%, which although not much more than a pass, seems to me encouraging.

Also this morning I received word that my baggage was shipped on the Caledonian, which unfortunately is going to Glasgow. Of course when I was booking the baggage I thought I would be going to Edinburgh, and so thought I was doing something very smart by sending it to Glasgow. Now I will have the expense of bringing it down by rail.

As you see I still have the typewriter, but I am expecting this week to have some offers for it. I have advertised it together with several other items that I feel are non-essentials. I have definitely asked the Lord that if I am meant to sell them at this time, it may be without undue loss of the original amount invested. If I do not get a good offer for them, I will not sell just at the moment, but will keep an eye on the wanted column and try to sell them that way.

I have been thinking a good deal about the heavy costs. Providing that I do not fail, and go straight through the six years, the annual cost will be something like this:

Cost of board and living: 208 pounds
Cost of fees and books: 75 pounds

I realize that you have been more than generous to me in the past, and only feel ashamed that I have not made more careful use of what you have given me.

I am able to stay on here at the hostel. Dr. Bennett has not said very much to me as yet. Being English they are all very reserved, and it is quite difficult to know what one's exact position is. I feel sure however that I will be able to stay on here as long as I like.

I will be only too glad to get the shoes for you. I only wish I could do more for you. I hope that you do not feel under any obligation to send me a definite amount of money, as I may have given you the impression, or in fact any money at all. I think we can trust that if this thing is of God, that if you cannot, then the Lord will show other channels through which the need will be supplied. I would not be at all happy to know that I had been the means of you working harder than you should, not getting the needed holidays or relaxation and thereby shortening your life. I think it would be a great deal better if you did not send any cash and took it easier, so that I could have the benefit of your friendship and advice for as long a period as the Lord permits. See what you think.

By the way, do you know any details of our family tree? The office for looking such things up is just handy and it would be interesting to see what the Harpers of old used to do.

Much love, Howard

127 Karangahape Road
Auckland, N.Z.
November 18th 1954

My dear Son

Yours of the 10th arrived yesterday, for which many thanks. We are so glad that you can stay on at the M.M.A. hostel, and hope you continue to have a single room. It would surely be wise to pay extra to have the quietness for study which means so much to you.

I hope your baggage comes safely by the Caledonian per Glasgow, and that nothing is missing. Of course I'm waiting to see how the Lord works in providing a hospital opening for you.

Guess you would not find much of worth at the Family Tree Factory! On the Harper side, my great grandfather, Edwin Harper, was captain in the First Life Guards. His son, Albion, my grand-father, was educated to follow in the same line. But he disgraced himself by marrying Catherine Blyth, of Chirnside near Berwick on Tweed. Catherine was the daughter of Betty Blyth, queen of the Scottish gypsies, whose gravestone I have a kodachrome slide of.

My mother was Esther Gatland, daughter of William Gatland, a small country brewer of Oxted. He was converted later in life through reading an address by CHM, on "the dying thief". He sold up everything at a loss, and moved to Brighton, where he died in his early 60's of heart trouble.

Now a word regarding finance again – I appreciate your thought for me, son, but there is no need to worry about being a burden. The amount I am putting aside for you is pretty well what I have been using for the Lord's work each year for awhile now.

It is a good thing to have some incentive to work for; things were getting too easy at the shop, and I began to feel like an old man, not much to look forward to in business, but the end. Now that Selwyn has left and I have had to keep closely to work, it has been good for me and given me a fresh interest to feel that I am needed about the place. I am so thankful, too, that I can share with you and have a part in preparation for future service for Him.

You say you are not physically tired enough to drop off to sleep at bedtime. This is a warning signal to avoid late study; the beginning of sleeplessness leads to inefficiency, later to nervous strain, then more sleeplessness. Finish by nine, have a smart walk, hot drink and to bed. If walking alone at night, you will remember to keep to the outer edge of the footpath so that none can approach you unseen. If a woman accosts you, don't answer, go for your life. If you stop, she may shriek and call an accomplice near at hand, who would swear you had insulted her. Not too easy to prove one hasn't, in a police court if there are two witnesses against you.

Much love from
Dad

Gravestone of Catherine Blyth,
daughter of Betty Blyth.

M.M.A.
31 Bedford Place
London W.C.1
12th June 1955

Dear Dad

Well, the day I have been working for seven months, arrives tomorrow. Remembering the blank ignorance of that time, I can give thanks for the progress made, and that at least a sketchy outline of what I am supposed to know, I do know. Last night, close to midnight, I realized that I have now done all the study I could possibly do.

If the worst really does happen and I fail the exams, then the Botany teacher assures me that it will be a comparatively easy matter to revise for the November Exams.

June 19th – Last week I had a note from Mum; written on the back of a telegraph form (this seems to be her favourite correspondence medium). She was in Perth and had been going for a tour of the city. I say, by the time Mum gets here she'll be a new woman. Traveling first class! I wonder how she is enjoying first class travel. On the "Strathmore" all the first class folk dressed up in evening dress for supper. In my wildest dreams I really cannot see Mum in an evening frock, though "wonders will never cease".

I am looking forward to the arrival of Mum. I trust I will be a help to her, and show a grace that I am afraid is often lacking. I hope she has made some plans as I'm quite hopeless at making plans for other people.

If I am going to get this into the post by 2:30pm (posts are all closing earlier due to the rail strike) I had better close.

All my love
Howard

Mum and friend, ready for a swim,
Browns Bay, Auckland.

50

31 Bedford Place
London W.C.1
26th June 1955

Dear Dad

You will be glad to know that Mum has arrived safely. I was able to meet the train and I trust made her arrival a little easier than it would have been otherwise.

Fortunately the boat did not arrive at Tilbury until 2:30pm. I was able to telegraph in between my two exams of that day and say I would meet the train at St. Pancras at 7:15pm.

Today I went to Welbeck Hall with her, and afterwards came back to the MMA for lunch. The Bennett's asked us to a cup of tea after lunch. I then took Mum to see the London Hospital, after which I meant to take her to the Parliament buildings. However I made a mistake, and after a long time discovered the bus was going in the wrong direction. So I quite successfully destroyed any reputation I might have had with Mum, of knowing London.

On this bus trip a rather unpleasant fact emerged. From what I could make out, reading between the lines, Mum's idea in coming across was not so much to see England or me (though these no doubt play a part), but because she feels frustrated. She sees the years slipping by and does not seem to be gaining the love and respect of her husband. Nor does she seem to be gaining the chief rallying point – the brick house. So as a gesture of semi-defiance/ semi-challenge, she takes this trip to England hoping to leave things stew for a time.

It is a difficult question, and I must confess that humanly speaking I see no answer to it. I realize, perhaps, that unwittingly you might have wronged Mum, and that she has wronged you. The fact is, over the years your interests have drawn apart, so that there is extremely little common ground which you can share. Though from the human angle things look gloomy, from the Christian angle there is unlimited hope, and problems like this are an encouragement to ask of God the impossible. Personally I am of the opinion, that Mum is ready to take some new steps of faith.

The exams have been wending their weary way onwards. Last week saw the practical of the Cambridge Papers and two London theory papers. I am hopeful that I have scraped through the practical, but wonder about the theory.

The weather at the moment is very hot and sticky, far too hot to study. Not a very good frame of mind with which to approach the new study for Physics and Chemistry, I'm afraid.

Well, I must sign off and drop this in the post box.

All my love, Howard

127 Karangahape Road
Auckland New Zealand
July 17th 1955

Dearest Son

I have given some thought to your letter of June 26th, written just after Mother had arrived and have wondered just how much or how little to say in reply.

You correctly interpreted, I think, the motive in making the journey overseas. You would perhaps scarcely realize that I am grieved that you realize it is not just for your sake, and that she has revealed this.

Frustration, I think, is the right word. And it seems that some explanation is due to you, as it has already been given to Blyth, so that you may learn if possible from our mistakes! Please realize that what follows is by way of explanation, not of blame for Mother or vindication of myself. I have no wish to do either.

To many who know her, but not to herself, it has been obvious that her passion for "outside interests" – school, apartment houses, jobs, houses, money etc. – has been the outcome of frustration along the lines of our relationship. She resented being "just a wife and mother", not realizing that it could be the call of the Lord and, as such, the most honorable way to serve Him. From there it was an easy step to begin to shape her way of life to suit her self, and to reckon she was getting her prayers answered. Now that the opportunities of being a wife and mother have departed, she is finding the reaping of the years of sowing not so satisfying.

No doubt I have failed miserably as a husband, and as a successful business man – the latter because I have not set my heart on making money or acquiring possessions. When I realized the disappointment of marriage desires, I too had to find an outlet. It drove me to an almost desperate devotion to God, and a cultivation of the awareness of His presence to such a point that I really do not know what loneliness is. I have had to think my own thoughts so much, that I can spend any amount of time alone, yet conscious that He is there. Some of the holidays I have spent thus have been days of heaven on earth, He has been so precious.

On the human side, you boys have been inexpressibly dear to me; the love that could have been Mother's has been poured out on you. Today I am reaping in mercy my countless prayers for you both. In many ways I "mothered" you both. Had we been truly one, you would have known a father's care as father, and a mother's love as mother, which would have been normal and happier for you. How sad I am that you have suffered through our mistakes! Now you have both gone from the nest, never to return, and we can do nothing about it but take the whole thing to Him to deal with us according to His own will.

So perhaps, dear son, you can realize for me the cycle of frustration has just about completed its course. Failures and disappointments are recognized and mourned; pride is utterly in the dust. Yet because of His Cross, I have found not only forgiveness, but present rest and peace. There may be a few struggles ahead yet, age brings its distresses, but at the center, He is there, and where He is, there is rest and peace.

For Mother, the way is still of frustration. Neither arguments, voyages of discovery, or even brick houses and gadgets would dissolve it. If she would take everything- herself, with her frustration, possessions, desires and plans to Him at the Cross, He could adjust her and restore the years the locust has eaten.

I feel that she will not take the word from us, we are too closely involved. She is in the school of God, and He is able to speak in His own way. For this we are all praying.

Much love to you from
Dad

Howard at the beach, age four.

Howard, age five or six, Mt. Eden, Auckland,
and with his dog Barney, age eleven.

M.M.A.
31 Bedford Place
London W.C.1
15th August 1955

Dearest Dad

Today is rather a special day. I heard today from the Cambridge board that I had passed in Botany and Zoology. You will remember that I sat these subjects under both the Cambridge and London Boards. Cambridge always get their results out first.

I very nearly cabled you, but did not on sober reflection. The fact is, unless I have achieved some sort of pass in Religious Knowledge then I will have to sit the whole lot again. However if I find I have passed then I will cable you immediately.

Under the Cambridge board, I passed Zoology with a narrow

but safe margin. In the case of Botany, I was much closer to the border line. I failed in the practical, due to cutting a bad section of the material, but passed in the theory papers. That evidently gave me enough marks to pull through.

Had Robbie's circular today. It was very interesting. They are really getting down to work these days. One thing that no doubt Robbie has learned is that girls are easier to handle than boys. His two new "Miss Sahibs" seem to be settling down well. Of course they come from his culture, which makes for easier relations.

I must say my mind feels a good deal easier after hearing the news from Cambridge this morning. You know how it is; you unconsciously build up quite an anxiety state waiting for the wretched results. In fact it was as good as a holiday to me. If I have managed all three, it is the first and hardest step in breaking into the medical profession, with absolutely no background in these studies!!! Well I must get to bed!

Love
Howard

OVERSEAS TELEGRAM

+ PASSED ALL THREE THANKS BE TO GOD + HOWARD ++

Chapter 3
The Cost

Mother and Monika.

Back at MMA

Monday 13th Aug. 1956

Dearest Dad

Last Monday we left Kate, and went across to Edinburgh. On the way we called in at Shott's, and by pure accident met some of the Neil's, relations of Mum's family. No doubt she has told you all about it. We picked up my mail in Edinburgh and that afternoon pressed on through Berwick late into the night, until we stopped just out of Doncaster. Mum did not wish to spend money on "these bed and breakfast places", so we "slept" in the car on the last day of our trip. Mum did not sleep a wink of course, and in all I only slept a couple of hours. Next morning we were up early and arrived back in London in the afternoon.

I have reached the conclusion that it is just about impossible to take Mum on any sort of holiday that involves hotels. She hates the continual handout it involves. Funny to say though, on her arrival back in London, she has taken a job as Assistant Manageress to quite a posh private hotel in Swiss Cottage. I don't doubt that she is getting dug in for a very lengthy stay in these parts.

On our return on Tuesday, I went into action clearing up all the accumulated junk of the First MB. It has taken some days to get all my stuff in order and to get organized for the Second MB.*

As you say, I have been quietly thinking over the different hospitals, and it seems that the choice lies between the Middlesex and University College Hospital (UCH). From what I have discovered, I think it will be easier to get through Second MB at UCH.

---

* The First MB was a one year course in basic sciences that was a prerequisite for acceptance into university for the study of medicine. The Second MB was taken after one and a half years of preclinical studies.

Their anatomy is much more generalized than any other London Hospital. Between Middlesex and UCH there is not much difference in the physiology teaching, both excel in this field. I am still making enquiries about the anatomy teaching at the Middlesex. I am not thinking in terms of Second MB, but in terms of Primary FRCS (Fellowship Royal College of Surgeons), for this is my long term project. I believe that if I have this goal firmly before me from the very outset of my studies it will help me to study carefully during my Second MB work, and not try to slide over anything.

I enclose a rough draft of my circular letter; you might want to take a look at it.

Love Howard

Medical Missionary Society
31 Bedford Place, London
England
August 1956

My dear praying friends

One of you wrote to me recently to say that "Every day your name, with that of Colin Blair, is remembered before the Throne of Grace". This letter is to thank you for your remembrance and to say that any good I have done, or anything achieved in Christ's name through the past year, has been as a result of the faithfulness of God and in answer to your many prayers.

It was a very happy moment when after the recent exams I saw my name on the notice board outside the University of London as having completed the First MB. After having a second look at the board to make sure it was really true, my first thought was to share the good news with my father, who has faithfully stood by me in every way during this very uphill climb.

Looking back, I am more than ever conscious that it was God's grace alone that enabled me. The standard of the examinations is very high as they are designed to prevent too many people entering the medical faculties. As most of you know, prior to coming to England I had never before looked at Physics, Chemistry or Biology, and had no real interest in them. I now leave the pure science subjects behind and plunge into the more interesting side of medical studies, Anatomy and Physiology. For the sake of others whom God may be calling to do equally difficult tasks, I would like to testify that His callings are His enabling, and that despite any apparent lack of talent, if He really calls then no mountain is high enough to prevent the working out of His will.

Since that happy day when the results came out, I have been having a break, and together with Mother have been exploring Scotland.

Perhaps you will be wondering what the future holds for me now that I have passed this exam, and for what to pray in this regard. In October I commence dissection in one of the London Hospitals; I have the choice of three to which I may go. This is a most important and interesting part of my medical studies and with other aspects of Anatomy and Physiology will keep me busy for about one and a half years; then I must again face the examiners, this time for the Second MB. The third and final section comes three years after that. You can see that there is a pretty full programme of study before me for the next four and a half years.

I am always glad to hear from any of you. Colin Blair continues to write regularly to me and I know that you are joining with me in prayer that God will bless Colin and Gladys and the preaching ministry which he is beginning to exercise. Mother continues to keep well, and as ever, busy.

With my sincere regards to you all,
Ever Yours in Christ,
Howard F. Harper

127 Karangahape Road
Auckland New Zealand
August 28th 1956

Dear Son

Yesterday also brought an air-letter from Mother, telling of the holiday – which she seems to have enjoyed BECAUSE of the fish and chips (!), also telling of her new job with the Jewess. As before, I shall make no comment when writing to her; unless she meets the Lord in the way, anything else is of little consequence.

Your circulars have all been posted, and I enclose a copy for your approval. I made very few changes this time, mostly omissions or the recasting of a phrase to avoid awkwardness.

So glad that you met Robbie in London, and hope you are able to get him an opening at the Golder's Green Assembly to tell of the work. I've put aside his circular with the intention of dropping him a note. Maybe by the time you have your medical degree he will have changed his opinion about your trip from Karachi.

Well, it is time I stopped, nearly five o'clock. The shop is very quiet this week, school holidays on. I'm to go to Chenery's for tea, and then on to Eden Hall for ministry.

Much love from
Dad

Stanley Harper – father of Howard.

M.M.A.
32 Bedford Place
London WC1
5th Jan 1958

Dearest Dad

Thank you again for your latest letter. You will have heard how Christmas passed with me. I do regret the way the last two or three Christmases have been spent – pure self-indulgence and unnecessary overeating. Still, things are not altogether under my control. I am trying to give Mum pleasure and I have a sneaking suspicion she is trying to do the same to me, though neither of us would ever admit it, I'm sure!

This past week I have been plowing on through Physiology in fine style. I have practically covered the main sections of Physiology and this is very gratifying, as it means that I will be able to put more time into anatomy during term time. We will have a good revision course (for the Second MB exams).

Apart from this, I have been restocking with clothes at the annual sales now in progress. I have bought another suit, gray, single breasted, which will be suitable for clinical work and also more underwear, a shirt, socks and ties.

Today I'm at Stock, a village in Essex, spending the day at our Christian Union house party. It is in a beautiful mansion, owned by Westham Central Mission. It makes Eastern Beach look rough. Weather is cold but bracing. I have handed over my last job as President of the Christian Union – rather thankfully.

I'm expecting to go to a Central Asian Society Meeting on Wednesday – "Big game hunting, on the roof of the World" – it should be fun. One of the boys from the hostel will be coming with me.

Colin wrote an interesting letter and he seems in good spirits.

With much love
Howard.

Killaha
Kermane
Co. Kerry EIRE
30th March 1958

Dearest Dad

As you can see from the address, I have fled away from London to more peaceful surroundings.

I came here on Thursday, together with John Hunt – he also failed. Together we have been eating, sleeping and trying (successfully) to forget about our recent disappointment.

Well, I'm sure the news came as a disappointment to you, as it did to me. Before I came over here, I enquired which parts of the Second MB exam I had failed. I was not surprised to find that Biochemistry was responsible for the failure. It seems very mean to be failed on a potty little subject like that, and I still don't feel they were quite fair about it.

What it does mean is that next time my chances of passing are very favorable. I was told that there is every chance of my passing next time. The irritating thing is the time and money wasted in the meantime, just when I should be going full steam ahead into clinical work. However, God must have a purpose in this delay. We committed this into His care and His plan cannot be changed – even by crackpot biochemists.

I should be thankful for this extra three months in which to really revise and understand many of the basic things in Anatomy

Students of the Medical Missionary Association.

and Physiology. I mean to use them in this way and not merely to "cram" my way through an exam!

Term starts two weeks after Easter, and the re-take exam is about the 8th or 10th of June, so this does not leave a great deal of time for revision.

When I came over here I felt at the end of my tether – the strain of the two and a half weeks of exams and then the disappointment at the result. Somehow, I didn't feel disappointed for myself, but for you and the other folks I know are interested. But now I feel much better and in fact am looking forward to getting back to work again.

Spring is just coming to these parts, and we are having a sunny day (our first!!). A lady, who lives nearby, cleans the house and cooks our evening meal, leaving us free the rest of the day.

Sorry I failed.

With much love
Howard

127 Karangahape Road
Auckland New Zealand
April 8th 1958

Dearest Son

In Mother's air-letter last week she mentioned you had gone to Ireland, so I was not surprised this morning to receive a green air-letter from you!

Without exception everyone here has been thankful to hear you got the partial pass, and thought you did well to do it in the time, so you have no need to reproach yourself. After all, we did leave it in the

Lord's hand, and I am quite sure it will turn out for the best. It seems a bit potty of the Biochemistry boys to "queer the pitch", but I suppose to them it is the most important subject in the whole exam.

It looks to me like a kindly intervention to give you a break before the final three years of clinical, when I understand you will not get the number of longer term breaks that 'varsity gives. What you know of Physiology and Anatomy is the groundwork of what you will use for the rest of your life, so it may as well be more than just scraping through. As mentioned before, if you think it advisable, get extra coaching in Biochemistry.

Blyth has just been in, and his reading of your letter makes us think you have all subjects to sit again in June. I did not realize you would only have a couple of months for revision. Don't allow yourself to get stale and weary.

Blyth is taking a month of gospel meetings at Birkenhead. He is developing as a speaker, and is much in demand.

Time I got to bed so will close. The Lord bless you son, and keep you fresh and fit for the June exams.

Much love from
Dad

M.M.A.
31 Bedford Place
London W.C.1
11th July 1958

Dearest Dad

Many thanks for your cable received a few minutes ago. It was a comfort to me. His way IS perfect, but at times like this one is often tempted to not be able to see any reason for it all.

I am just away to Keswick convention for the week. After casting around, I decided that this was the best thing to do. If I went away for a holiday on my own, I might tend to get depressed. Staying with a crowd of lads at the IVF (Intervarsity Fellowship) camp should be a good antidote for anything like that. Also the quietness of the hills, and the godly atmosphere should give the Lord some better chance to speak to me.

I must say the news came as a most unwelcome surprise to me. Right until the viva in Anatomy I had thought that although I might be close in Anatomy, I should be able to pull through. However, the viva did not go at all well, I did not seem to say a right word, and then I knew that trouble lay ahead.

I talked the matter over with Dr. Aitkin, the Christian man who is responsible for the anatomy teaching (though he did not fail me, it was the external examiner from Manchester who did that). He advised me to go for the Conjoint Examination in September and try to get into the West London Hospital. This is a smaller hospital which allows students to study for Conjoint.

I went to see them the next day. Though they were very sympathetic, the outlook for starting in October, presuming I pass in September, is not very hopeful. I must now wait until the Sub Dean of University College comes back from holiday. It may well be that I should go back to University College and repeat the second M.B. next March.

So once again the future is uncertain. Whether they will let me come back to University College is also doubtful, although they have done so quite often in the past.

One thing has crystallized out in my mind, and that is that I must now give up all thought of Ruth. I have written to her and told her so. I know she will not be too upset about it, as the other lad has been getting some encouragement from her lately – he now has a clear field.

Well, I must drop everything and finish packing for the camp. Before I do so, I must say that I am really sorry this has happened, for I know the unhappiness and expense it will be to you.

With all my love, yours as ever, Howard

127 Karangahape Road
Auckland
July 18ᵗʰ 1958

Dearest Son

Yours of the 11ᵗʰ came this morning, and I am thankful to hear you are having a break at Keswick, even though the weather there is so often very wet.

My cable urging a proper holiday would arrive while you were away, but you would get it on your return. I do think you have reached the stage where you need a break for a few weeks from books to the out of doors. It would be false economy to drive yourself to utter weariness, the Lord does not expect it of us, and you would do better work more happily if feeling fresh and fit.

The uncertainty regarding the future is something I cannot resolve, as I do not know all the circumstances or possibilities. I can only suppose that the idea of Conjoint is so that you can begin hospital work in October.

If that is possible and you begin clinical studies in October, would you also intend sitting Second MB again next March? Revision alongside all the new clinical work would be a heavy program of study, and for that reason you would need to keep as fit as possible.

Does this miss mean that UCH may withdraw your studentship with them and leave you to find another hospital? I feel so helpless about it all, away out here, but hope Dr. Torrens will be able to advise you as to the wisest action under the circumstances.

A fond parent would gladly have saved you from the disappointment of delay, but a wiser Father has some better thing ahead.

Colin and Gladys are due here on Tuesday, and I am deputed to voice the welcome of the assembly at the meeting in the evening. I've not yet got the word for the occasion.

Much love from
Dad

31 Bedford Place
London W.C.1
Sun. Oct. 20th 1958

Dearest Dad

It is one of those rather typical quiet, gray days of the English autumn. The leaves are dropping off the trees without even turning brown. I suppose they had so much water this summer that it would take a long time to dehydrate them to their autumn tints. Already the temperature has dropped, though it is still not too cold and I am able to go around without a pullover.

No doubt you are wondering just what my first impressions of the West London Hospital are. I must say, on the whole they have been good. They are keen to teach and do not mind how much time you put in on the wards. In fact they invited us to attend outside of the usual hours, which is unheard of in the other teaching hospitals. The food in particular is excellent and cheap. Teaching is carried on in the Fulham and West London Hospitals; all together they must total about 700 beds. The Hammersmith district is poor and rough, and has been the scene of a good deal of the race rioting.

The introductory course is carried on at a very gentle pace compared with the Second MB course I have just finished. Unfortunately, the stethoscope I bought in Melbourne, while on the missionary medical course there, is not of the approved type. So it looks as if I will have to spend the money and get one of the approved types.

Robbie Orr replied briefly to my recent letter to him, and gave news of a big split in some of the meetings in the Punjab. Some dispute between the elders and the full time brothers, so that in the three places there are two groups meeting, including Multan. Well, well, human nature seems to be the same the world over. As intractable and stubborn as ever!

Word came from the bank of 191-1-9d. Many thanks for this fresh provision. As I mentioned before, I found this last quarter more expensive than anticipated – I guess it was the extra exam fees!

With much love
Yours Howard

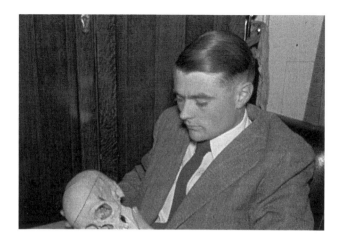

Howard went on to win a prize in anatomy.

31 Bedford Place
London W.C.1
15th May 1959

Dearest Dad

I have just returned from a rather hot and trying day at the West London, and have received your letter with real interest.

As you say, the past few weeks have not been without their movement, even if only the restlessness of my own spirit! I have been conscious for a long time that a change is needed, some new vista to open up. Since passing the second M.B. (March 1959), I have felt remarkably restless and unsettled. However, the mass of evidence seems to be building up that there must be no move for me, at least as far as hospitals is concerned. I saw the Sub Dean of University College yesterday (a communist I think, but he has always been very kind to me) and he strongly advised sticking to the West London. In fact nobody seems keen for me to go back to N.Z., except me! The only open alternative is in fact N.Z., and the more I think about it, the less likely it seems they will allow me credit for the clinical work I have done here. As the UCH man said to me, in two years time I will be starting to sit my finals here.

The time has come to say a word about a new factor on our horizon. For some months now I have been conscious that the long drawn out wait for the right partner to come along is coming to an end. This time I have waited for some time, to quietly prove whether or not it really is the answer.

Over a year ago a new girl came over from Germany to help in the running of the M.M.A., and learn English at the same time. Her name is Monika Pshichholz, and she was born in the North of Germany, on the border between Poland and Germany. Her mother and father are both dead. Her mother disappeared during the war, taken by the Russians towards Siberia. Her father died about 1955 from heart trouble. Monika has in fact been brought up first by a German General and his wife living near Hamburg, then more latterly by German deaconesses. They in turn put her in touch with the Hospital for Tropical Diseases in Tubingen, near the Swiss border of south Germany. There she did her preliminary training for her nursing course. She came over here with the intention of learning English for a time at the M.M.A. and then to take up nursing training.

She became a Christian after much grief and struggle when she was 14-15. Before this time she was in touch with the Roman Catholics, as her mother was a R.C. Her father was nominally Lutheran. In the small village she was living at the time, the most Christian group were the Lutherans, so in her new found faith she turned to them, but has remained curiously unattached to them.

From the first time I saw her I felt her to be a girl out of the ordinary, certainly as far as looks and charm goes. Of course, she didn't have very much English then, so some months had to pass before I could get to know her at all. Eight months ago she started nursing at Moorfields eye hospital, and has got on extremely well there. The Matron, the other nurses and the patients thoroughly approve of her. She was able to lead to Christ an English girl who shared her room.

About her faith, I am sure it is thoroughly founded on Christ and the Bible and has been personally beaten out through much hardship and suffering. She is 19 years of age, but despite the age gap between us there is a singleness of heart and purpose that I have not felt before. Her idea of taking up nursing was for missionary service. She was not quite sure of where, but had thoughts of India. The important thing is that the Lord has spoken to her and called her to Himself and His service, the place is not so important.

She is one of the few girls I have known, Christian or Non-Christian, who has that natural simple charm that wins the hearts of all she comes in contact with. This is why Dad I feel, that for her sake as well as for mine, you will overlook the more obvious difficulties of nationality, age, etc. I will introduce her to Mother, who I know will be genuinely glad to know her.

I know that you will join me in prayer unceasing, that if this is to be , it will be God's victory, despite my many past and present mistakes, and will be the maximum blessing both for ourselves, but especially for the need of the world, for God's kingly rule.

Your own problem about coming over here, I have been well aware of. I rather hope that the new event will also in some way prove a blessing to Mother, and clear the way for you to come over here in due course, if we cannot come over to N.Z. that is. (My friendship with Monika is completely between ourselves and one or two friends, at the moment.)

Very much love
Yours Howard

31 Bedford Place
London W.C.1
2nd June 1959

Dearest Dad

I'm sorry that my last two letters seemed so contradictory. I cannot help being what I am, and by now you know fairly well that the "am" is mixed up with a great deal of "I", which at times steps to the forefront and tries to assume control. I have been very conscious of the strife and turmoil generated in the last couple of months as I have turned this way and that.

Rationally, I suppose the fact that I have been stuck at what the world would call a 'second best' hospital has evoked this strong withdrawal phobia. It is no doubt the strong streak of pride, as well as the desire to have the best available, that has sent me casting around in the feckless manner that has so rightfully upset you. I have not heard from the N.Z. authorities, but there seems no doubt about it at all, that I should stick on here in London. No doubt it would be more pleasant in N.Z. but London seems to offer the best and earliest chance to get qualified and that should be the main consideration. Instead of kicking at the West London, I should in fact thank God for it, and accept it as His best. I have not quite come to this position yet, and this is the main cause of the trouble.

One thing I am especially sorry about is that somehow Monika should have been introduced into all this confusion. She deserves a good deal more than to be mixed up in what after all may well prove to be one of the more ephemeral of my daydreams. She, more than London or Dunedin, will determine the shape of my future usefulness both to God and man. To her, will be entrusted the bearing, and to a large part, the bringing up of our descendants. I have

74

given a great deal more thought than in the past, to the question of the right partnership. Now that the end seems in sight, it seems a pity that I have tangled it up with this other question, so that you have not been able to join in my own rejoicing to any great extent. I hope that circumstances will work out that you will be able to come over to London and see her for yourself. Then, I feel sure that you will agree, that even if your son is a bit feckless with his choice in medical schools (no doubt the London Hospital should have been my first choice, rather that UCH), that he has at last picked a winner for his wife.

Well, I won't say any more about it only that in due course I will take a photo of Monika, so that you will be able to get some sort of idea what she looks like.

I draw to a close. Weather at the moment is truly beautiful, just enough rain to keep the grass green.

With very much love
Yours Howard

Monika in Tubingen,
Germany.

127 Karangahape Road
Auckland New Zealand
June 12th 1959

Dearest Son

It is Friday again, cold and wintry with some fitful sunshine, so our side of the street is not too busy, and I'll try to get a letter away to you, though it may be with some interruptions.

Now about the West London; all along I have realized your disappointment at being confined to that, when you so much wanted to be at UCH. It would have been nice to have gone through with some of the earlier associates, and to have had the advantage of the best place to train. I have also thought of the discomfort of being with the others at the hostel who are at historical hospitals, whilst you are where there is probably no tradition and little prestige. It is no consolation to think that perhaps you may have been at UCH now, but for the distraction of time and attention that Ruth occasioned, and on the other hand it is no use crying over spilt milk. Yet having said that, you will understand my concern that you may allow yourself to be distracted, either with swapping around colleges or with Monika, and thus lose another year of precious time.

Would it not be better to realize that unless the LORD is opening a door on His own account, without your wrangling things, the present door is His open door of opportunity? I know nothing about West London, except what you have told me; yet if the teaching is reasonably adequate and the clinical material sufficient, I do not see why you should not get all you need there.

Yes, your future may be influenced by Monika much more than you realize. When you write about the future family and their upbringing, I naturally wonder how far things have gone. Does she look on you with favor? Is she thinking in terms of engagement and marriage? When? Has she any thoughts of Pakistan or Central Asia? Is she likely to see things in an Assembly pattern? What are her plans for training? And so on. If she is not clear on these things, your plans for the future might be better left for the future, whilst you attend to the next thing. Otherwise, it may be just more castles in the air, and so much waste of time.

Have you said anything yet to Mother about Monika? Of course I'm singing dumb here.

Time I got back to the bench so will close with much love.

From Dad

Howard's Academic Hurdles:

- *General Certificate of Education (GCE) passed August 1955*
- *First M.B. (a basic science course and requirement for entrance to Medical School) passed August 1956*
- *Second M.B. (exam taken after the first two years at medical school) failed twice, passed March 1959*
- *M.B.B.S. (Bachelor of Medicine & Bachelor of Surgery – the qualification received after five years of medical school and one year practical training) and Conjoint M.R.C.S., L.R.C.P passed 1961*
- *Diploma of Ophthalmology (D.O.) passed 1967*
- *Fellow of the Royal College of Surgeons (F.R.C.S.) passed 1970*

Mr. Howard Harper, M.R.C.S., L.R.C.P., M.B.B.S., D.O., F.R.C.S. – quite a mouthful!

Chapter 4
Two are Better than One

Monika receives her Ophthalmic Nursing Diploma from Moorfields Eye Hospital.

127 Karangahape Road
Auckland New Zealand
June 5th 1960

Dearest Son

Either my letter record is wrong, or else I've not posted one to you since May 23rd! It seems unbelievable that nearly a fortnight has elapsed without my writing.

No, I guess your New Zealand stomach is not ready for sauerkraut & pork – very strong fare; it reminds one of the Maori delicacy, pork bones and *puaha*. Cabbage is not the easiest at any time, but pickled etc. it must be dynamite. Some things you will need to let Monika enjoy herself.

So you did give her the IVF commentary! Well it is a good one, but I guess she will need to take it in small doses at first. Like many Germans, she has done marvelously to acquire such a good grip of the English language. But as I said before, all her thinking will be coloured by her native tongue, and though she may later learn to think in English, in her inner life I would expect her to think in German, and that for long enough the Lord will speak to her in the language of her own dear German Bible.

Well, after all that I have said, you will think I'm getting soft in the head, when I tell you I'm likely to be over with you for your wedding! I'll tell you the story when I come, and of course I'm looking forward to seeing you and Monika very much.

Considering the high cost of the fares, I think I may as well get a little holiday out of the trip too, as I am never likely to come again. So I propose to leave here very soon – you will not have time to reply to this, as I should leave here by the 14th and I will come the Pacific route by air; spending two days in Honolulu, San Francisco and New York to get sleep and rest, so that I do not land in Britain like a corpse.

The day I decided to come, the text calendar read "My Presence shall go with Thee, and I will give Thee rest." Though I dread the journey and wonder why I'm leaving my comfortable little nest here, I'm resting in the assurance that He will undertake.

Though you will not have time to reply, I can write again giving details, and it will reach you in ample time as my journey takes over a week.

Meantime, much love from
Dad

P.S. Let me break the news to Mother myself. I'll try and write to her tomorrow. Bed time now.

127 Karangahape Road
Auckland New Zealand
June 12th 1960

Dear Son

It is difficult for me to collect my wits for writing; there has been so much to do in just a few days.

I think I mentioned leaving here on the evening of Tuesday the 14th, with the expectation of arriving in London Tuesday 21st, but I do not yet know at what time. It will be an all night journey and I would be happiest if you yourself could get time off to meet me. I would much rather the others did not come; I guess my first wish will be for bed, not social pleasantries!

I shall also be grateful if you will book me in somewhere until I can get my feet.

Scarcely anyone here knows I am leaving. Alec Thorne will look after the house, sleeping here sometimes and airing the place. Blyth will cut the lawns.

Did you know Colin has lost his caravan? He was driving the outfit with another missionary, when they discovered the caravan behind was in flames. They had to hastily uncouple the jeep, and watch it burn to the ground. So far he has not succeeded in finding a house in Lahore, and Gladys and the twins are still with friends in Abbottabad.

Now I'll post this as I go the MSC – Richard Goodall speaking, he & wife and 2 children leave shortly for Japan.

Much love from
Dad

Colin and Gladys with their twins.

Norwich, England
30/6/60

Dearest Son

Just a brief note, to report our doings.

We had a leisurely and pleasant run through to Cambridge. The car is an Anglia, which has only done 500 miles. Quite comfortable and roomy enough for three;* the engine has no pep, so one travels along quietly at 30mph, which is alright for holiday purposes.

At Cambridge we found a Bed & Breakfast in Jesus Lane, opposite the college. The usual occupants are students who are now on holiday. The place is primitive in the extreme. Nothing in the house can be less than 60 years old; no hot water, no washbasins – instead a china basin and jug in the bedroom and a Dickens character to bring an enamel jug of hot water to the door at 7:30am with, "Your hot water, Sir."

Coming into Norwich late in the afternoon, we find there is an agricultural show on and accommodation limited. So we came to an outer suburb, Thorpe, where Ted and Lil have spent the night at one place and I am at another.

Later this afternoon we had a country run around the Broads. Naturally, though I am greatly enjoying the fresh air and country scenery, my mind is continually exercised to know what the Lord would have me do (concerning Mother). To forget would be rather like living in a fool's paradise. I want to be sensitive to His voice and if He calls for sacrifice, to be willing to make it.

We have had a good tea and are going for a walk along the river, and may possibly call to see the Grubbs later.

Much love, from Dad

---

* Ted and Lil, Stan's brother and sister-in-law

M.M.A.
31 Bedford Place
London W.C.1
4th July 1960

Dearest Dad

I'm so glad that you are having a pleasant run through the English countryside.

To go back to the time you left – it seems absolutely ages ago, but things seem to be moving so quickly at the moment. Monika enjoyed her time with you on Monday very much, and told me I had a "good Dad". This was no news to me; in fact it has been the big factor in my life, humanly speaking anyway. It shows how much better she is, for she could struggle out of the mire onto the upward way with almost only God to help her!

We have begun the rather formal things like registering with the local Registrars for Marriage, of Kensington and Holborn. It is necessary to give three week notice. We have also spoken to Mr. Luke up at the Hall (the one who gives the notices), and asked him to take the service. He was highly delighted and spoke of the honor we had conferred on him. He also suggested that we leave the catering arrangements in his hands for the time being – something we were more than glad to do.

I am hoping to get the invitations printed sometime this week. Should I send them to people in N.Z.? It seems an awful long way, and rather like cadging for presents, but people do feel left out if they don't get invites. What do you think?

The dress situation for Monika is not yet solved. All the stores have sales on and much junk on display. I accompanied Mum and Monika on their first trip which was quite unproductive.

I can realize how the intransigence of Mum must be continually in your mind, though I rather hope less so as the days pass. The Lord is dealing with her, and we can quietly leave it to Him.

I will possibly be doing a locum as a House Physician at the Mildmay Mission Hospital from the 16th to the 23rd of this month. After that I will seriously begin looking for a flat.

Well I must close now and see about getting wedding invitations printed.

With very much love to yourself, and to Aunty and Uncle,

Yours, Howard

22 Parfrey Street
London W.6
13th October 1960

Dearest Dad

It is a very great privilege indeed, that I may call you thus. It is an answer to my desire throughout the years to have a godly father and a loving friend, to whose advice it is worth listening. I never found such in my father or foster fathers and if any man used to ask me about my father, there was only one I knew, the Father of our Lord Jesus Christ.

Thank you so much for your letter. Dear Dad, I hope you are not too much concerned about me! In the first fortnight at London Bible College it seemed a bit of a strain, things sounded to me as spoken in a new language and I found it hard to take down any notes. I am beginning to settle now and housework seems to become a pleasant exercise in the afternoon.

If we are not going to any meetings or having visitors ourselves, we have made it a rule to study. Howard is now very good and I think he does about five hours reading every day. I hope that if he goes on faithfully, his knowledge of things will be sufficient for the examination.

It is now real autumn weather, rather clear but cold. The last leaves from the oak trees fall to the ground. Auntie Lil and Uncle Ted just escaped in time, I'm sure they will be glad to be back at home.

Hope you are well Dad and putting on soon any lost weight. Is your shoulder still causing trouble?

With much love
Monika

Wedding day at Bridge Lane Chapel, Golders Green, London
Bridesmaid, Monika's sister, Barbara.

22 Parfrey Street
London W.6
11ᵗʰ Jan. 1961

Dearest Dad

At last I have time and peace of mind to be able to sit down and write letters once more. By now you will have my cable telling the good news about the three subjects passed at Conjoint. I can still hardly believe it; it is too good to be true.

It seems a long time since I last wrote to you, but then it is a long time since I wrote any letters at all! First of all, thanks for the 5 pound note which has since gone into shillings for the gas and electric fires.

I have had a surprisingly easy time with my exams so far, the only time I got a bit pushed was in the Surgery clinical. The anatomy viva in the afternoon went very well, as did the Pathology at the Royal College of Surgeons. My goodness, what a moment of tension while we waited for the results! We had to troop up one by one as our number was called and be told personally if we had passed; if successful we went along one corridor, and if not, out into the night. My apprehension mounted as I saw a majority walking sadly away. The pass rate in the end was 22 out of 50. We all lined up before the examiners wearing their robes and trooped into a big room. Here we were given a little speech of congratulation, the examiners all bowed to us and filed out, with the mace bearer in front. I have six months to wait for the Medicine exam and I hardly know what to do for the next three months. The medical school secretary said, take a holiday!

I would say here, that I have been a bit anxious about Monika over the past week. We have been suspicious of a pregnancy the last seven weeks, and the day before I was due to sit the Pathology, she began to have all the signs of a miscarriage. I rushed off to the West London to have a chat with the consultant and his registrar had a look at her on Friday. He confirmed that it might in fact have been just the first stage of a miscarriage, and advised bed rest until bleeding ceased, also a test to determine if she was in fact pregnant. Last week it seemed that everything was happening at once. It was interesting that the next day I had to answer a question on miscarriage!! It seems for the moment that the danger of miscarriage is over. However it would be best not to make the pregnancy known until the question is settled one way or the other. That will be in 4-6 weeks time.

With much love
Your Howard and Monika

22 Parfrey Street
London W.6
13th March 1961

Dearest Dad

I had already typed out a letter to you yesterday, but so much has happened since then, it is not worth sending.

At 10:45am Monika had a miscarriage. I do not expect anything but a quite uneventful recovery to full health and strength, but we are taking it quietly. She ate a really good meal this evening; chicken supreme, beans, spinach (all deep freeze), followed by peaches and cream, tomato juice and yogurt. The best meal she has had for some time.

Monika is relieved to be free from the worry of the last few months. However, it is a sad thing for us. The future can never quite be the same, one cannot help wondering how the little life would have developed if it had been spared. Somehow the future seems just that little bit less worthwhile than it did when we had the prospect of a little one so soon, one's firstborn is always precious and looked for eagerly. The little thing was still living when it came out, but of course it was so unprepared for life outside of mother that it died even before it had lived. I expect we will have to wait until we get to Heaven to know him. However, there are no regrets, nor would we have it any different. Good and perfect is all that the Lord has done. Naturally we do not wish to advertise this; it is a private dealing between the Lord and ourselves.

The outline of things ahead is not all that clear – even as far as the holiday is concerned. We will be seeking the Lord's face for the steps ahead. The overall call remains Central Asia, the exact designation is not yet clear. Professionally speaking I would like to do a general medical, surgical and obstetric job, also eyes – each of these would take six months, but I'm hoping that some may be done in Pakistan.

I found it a struggle to finally cancel the booking for the plane down to Tangiers. We would have been leaving tomorrow night on holiday.

Well I guess that is about all, or rather about enough!

With very much love
Your Howard

127 Karangahape Road
Auckland New Zealand
March 23rd 1961

My dearest Howard and Monika

When I arrived from Tauranga this afternoon, the first thing I did was to run into town to see if there was any mail from you. You will know how grieved I am for you at the sad news yours of the 13th contained. I had hoped you both might have the joy of holding your firstborn in your arms. Because of the unsettled beginning, and the continuing hemorrhage, I was also a little apprehensive, and while committing you entirely to the Lord, had asked that if the little one was to be spared, it might be a normal and healthy child. To have the first child born with some disability would have been a sore trial indeed, and possibly one from which a Father's love has spared you.

If Colin and Gladys knew, they would fully understand how you feel, for their experience in losing their first was pretty acute; you will know how Colin must have felt when he had to carry the wee casket to the grave himself. It will not be all loss if it has drawn you closer together and given you new sympathy and understanding. Our faith is not really triumphant until we fully trust Him in the darkness, and can sing His praises when backs and perhaps hearts are sore and smarting. At the close of this note I will include a small poem from Fay Inchfawn. If you will carefully think through it I think you will both realize a little of the lasting gain, as well as the passing pain, of parenthood. My love and prayer is with you in this new experience.

"To a Little White Bird"

Into the world you came, and I was dumb,

90

Because "God did it", so the wise ones said;
I wonder sometimes "Did you really come?"
And "Are you truly ….dead?"

Thus you went out – alone and un-caressed;
    O sweet soft thing, in all your infant grace,
    I never held you in my arms, nor pressed
    Warm kisses on your face!

But in the Garden of the Undefiled,
    My soul will claim you … you, and not another;
    I shall hold out my arms, and say "My child"
    And you will call me "Mother!"

Now it is bedtime, so will close with most tender love,
from Dad

22 Parfrey Street
London W.6
27th March 1961

Dearest Dad

I was thinking a lot of you, as you were about to receive this sad news. I am so glad you had a little holiday before the letter. It is so great to know your understanding heart and sympathy and to receive the comforting words. Thank you too for sending the poem, they express the very thoughts which have run through my mind, they are very true words.

But are not all these things for a purpose? At the moment I cannot see it, but this gives the more reason to trust our sovereign God, who does all things well. I have found over the years that the more and dearer things the Lord took from me, the more grace and joy He gave. It is Christ himself who wipes away the tears and gently teaches us to submit ourselves to His will.

What a difference it is too, to be able to share a burden such as this. Howard has indeed been wonderful. He was everything at once. The Lord has indeed carried us through and we are looking to him for future guidance.

Unfortunately, I had told Mother and some of my people in Germany about it. It was just two days too soon. It would have saved me a lot of explaining, but who could tell? Mother came over to see us for a short time and gave us a proper old lesson, defending her own attitude in these matters.

The weather is still sunny, but generally much cooler.

I find it hard to type; it goes very slowly and also presents me with more spelling difficulties.

With much love
Monika

Monika on the steps of the M.M.A., London.

 # Chapter 5
The Journey

On the way to Central Asia – just outside of Ostend, Belgium.
Monika and Barbara, in front of the Land Rover and caravan.

1 Nelson St.
Hereford
3rd June 1962

Dearest Dad

It is hard to realize how quickly the time is flying by, with next to nothing done about our departure from England. So far, only the passports have been arranged.

17th June – As you can see I just have not been able to get back to the typewriter since starting this letter. Work at the hospital is certainly keeping me busy, as well as attending to all the other items.

Last week I closed the deal on a 1961 Land Rover, with a metal top and diesel engine. It has done 33,600 miles, but is in very good order and costs 605 pounds. Last weekend we went down to Burgess Hill to look at an 18 ft caravan. It is strongly constructed of welded tubular steel, furnished with two beds and two bunks, compact kitchen and toilet – ideal for living in, or a surgery. I have thought a lot about it and feel it is the best answer to the work ahead.

The problem at the moment is finance. As an investor I have turned out to be a complete failure. The unexpected plunge on Wall Street caught me napping with ¾ of our funds tied up in shares and we stand to lose a fifth of our original investment. According to Friday's prices on the stock exchange they are worth 873 pounds, and we have 300 pounds in cash from wages. Opposed to these assets are the following debts: 605 for the Land rover, 325 for the caravan, 430 for the cost of air travel from Pakistan to NZ and back, 70 for wayside expenses such as diesel on our overland trip to Pakistan. As you see these figures do not include any luxuries such as a fridge or anything.

We went down on Wednesday to receive the MRCS diploma at the College of Surgeons. We also put in all our heavy baggage to the shipping agent. It will be shipped to Karachi and held there until our return from New Zealand. We went out to Bridge Lane Chapel in the evening and I spoke briefly. They gave us a most warm reception and offered to accept responsibility for commendation with the N.Z. brethren and will give us a letter to this effect.

By the way Dad, here is something to keep under your hat. We have suspicions that you might turn out to be a quadruple Granddad. We are not saying anymore for the moment for we may turn out to be wrong.

You should see our little home now; practically everything has been shipped to Pakistan. I am glad we are leaving England now, for we will have such happy memories of it. All the grim slog will be forgotten, but we will not forget your continual care during all those long years.

With much love, your M&H

127 Karangahape Road
Auckland New Zealand
June 24th 1962

Dearest Son

The letter I sent yesterday from the shop probably reflected the disturbed state of mind in which it was written, and something of the concern I feel about your attitude to the arrangements you need to make for travel.

It seems that there are one or two things I should say, which I have refrained from saying, lest I hurt your feelings, but I ask you to give close attention to what is written and read it until you understand it.

FINANCE. In your budget you fail to allow for customs duty into Pakistan, insurances on goods sent and those that travel with you, and for any breakdown or unforeseen expenses you may meet. If you cancel the purchase of the caravan, it will leave you some money for emergencies – and there will be many.

DEBT. Whether you take the initial cost of the caravan 325 pounds, or what it will actually cost you with customs, insurance, and incidentals, 500 pounds; you are not justified in mortgaging the future. It would be unheard of for any society or missionary council to commend a worker who is 500 pounds (or much less) in debt. The stand of China Inland Mission is that an outgoing candidate should have, as the seal of his calling, sufficient to cover the cost of his outgoing, including kit. Without the caravan, you will barely have enough to see you through; with it, you will be about 500 pounds in debt.

TRAVEL. If you have not got ALL visas, you would do well to cancel your channel crossing until this has been done. It is just not possible to pass through these countries without visas in order.

IN GENERAL. It may be, son, that you have so set your heart on doing things regardless of the advice of those who care most for you, that you will ignore all we have said, and yet have an unexpressed thought in your subconscious mind that if worst comes to worst, you can always send a cable to Mum or Dad, and they will come to light with the cash. Mother has all her money tied up in four houses, and is trying to get some job in relief teaching for a few extra bob. So far as I am concerned, you are a married man in your thirties, and I expect you to avoid acting irresponsibly. You made sacrifices in hard work and grind to qualify; I made sacrifices that you know nothing about, to make it possible for you to do so. It should not be necessary for me to take up the load again. And if I am to be a mere 'sugar-daddy', I should not help but hinder your growth to maturity.

Needless to say, we look forward eagerly to you coming, and hope it will be a bright chapter in life for Monika.

Your ever loving, Dad

Bramloge U Varel,
Oldenburg
16ᵗʰ July 1962

Dearest Dad

It is a long time since I have written, our recent communications seem to have been in the rather expensive form of cablegrams!

On the Friday we set off from Hereford, I was busy in the casualty department until 3:30pm, amputating the little finger of a man with a nasty injury. With the help of the hospital porter we loaded up the Land Rover until it could hardly stagger, even then we had to leave behind our steel bookshelves at the last moment.

We arrived at the Spinks place to find that they had done most of the work on the caravan, except for one or two details. They loaded us down with kindness, giving us all sorts of useful things for the caravan. It was with great difficulty we tore ourselves away, leaving little time to make the journey to Dover. The trip itself proved to be a real testing ground for the brakes etc. The hill from Folkestone to Dover is really steep and I needed to change down into the reduction gears to get over it. We arrived in Dover 40 minutes before the boat sailed. I remembered your injunction about travel insurance against sickness and paid £5 for a three months comprehensive policy covering us both.

Landing at Calais gave no trouble and we were soon heading for the Belgium border and our first night on the road. We got over the border and stopped for the night by the side of the road. It proved to be a cold and disturbed night.

Germany – After many false starts we got onto our first autobahn and thus received the first big disappointment. The surface on it was terrible, just bump, bump the whole way. Except for short stretches, this has been true of all the autobahns. They are just completely worn out with the tremendous load of traffic they have carried for nearly thirty years and they have made little attempt to renew the badly smashed concrete. We were stopped by the police on the autobahn, and they absolutely shot everything to bits – verbally! I did not have the flashing lights connected to the caravan, my driving licence was not in order, I hadn't signed my insurance card, I did not have the right driving mirrors, and so it went on for over an hour. Finally they just drove away, leaving me wondering why they had bothered to stop me. We drove on and with difficulty found the flat of Monika's foster-mother's son. In stopping outside his house I backed into the car of someone who had driven up behind me. This cost me a good deal of trouble.

Next day we pressed on to Tubingen, up a very hilly road. Foolishly I left the caravan brakes on, so that by the time I found out some miles later, they were almost red hot. No serious damage seems to have been done. We chugged up the very steep slope to the Tropical hospital. On our way into the hospital we grazed a small car and scratched the paint on one side. The owner was furious and proceeded to take down all our insurance particulars. I wonder if we will hear any more of it. We have been overwhelmed with kindness during our stay here. Deaconess Hannah has always been a good friend to Monika and has really shown herself to be such during our stay here. In hundreds of little ways she has shown the love of Christ towards us.

We have both benefited from our stay here, and are getting quite brown from the hot sun. We have given thought to your comments regarding the caravan and feel it is too late now to look back. It is certainly on the heavy side but enormously strongly made and I am sure it will stand up well to the pounding which must lie ahead.

I think the money in hand will be enough to see us through the journey and back to New Zealand, provided there are no expensive repair jobs ahead.

Our route lies via Austria, Yugoslavia, Greece, Turkey, Syria, Lebanon, Jordan, Iraq, Iran, Afghanistan, and Pakistan. We will call at the British embassies in Belgrade, Amman (Jordan), Teheran, Kabul and Lahore.

Must close now, with apologies for the long delay in writing, which is entirely due to the great pressure of events.

With much love from us both
Yours
M & H

Monika says goodbye to many old friends and deaconesses,
Tubingen, Germany.

(Duplicate sent to
Amman)
127 Karangahape Road
Auckland, N.Z.
August 1ˢᵗ 1962

Dearest Howard

Of course we were all ever so glad to hear the first instalments of
"Pilgrim's Progress" as far as Tubingen, and await with breathless
interest the succeeding instalments. The few places you have given
to call at for mail make it difficult for us to do other than send
ahead, in hope that you will get the letters. As I am not sure how
long this will take to go from Tubingen to Belgrade, I am doing this
one in duplicate and will send one copy to Belgrade and the other
to the next address you gave, Amman in Jordan, though I should
think it will be some time before you reach the latter – if at all.

Yes, I think you will be naming your caravan "The Monster"
alright! It has given you a few anxious moments already, and as
unexpectedly rough the German roads have been, it is not likely
to be better on ahead. However you will learn by experience – the
dearest teacher one can have – not all can profit by the experience
of others; those who do save much labour and time.

My main concern is dear Monika; to think of the strain and
weariness of the bumping and engine noise, the heat and weariness, the nervous tension, just when I would that she was able to
travel quietly and happily, burdens me. She is a brave, dear girl and
however much it prolongs the journey you simply MUST put her
and the babe before your own wishes to press on, to go places and
see things.

You suggest arriving here by the end of September, but I think
you will have done well if you reach N.Z. by mid or late October.

I think as you face the way, you will discover the need to make haste slowly, to take it in easy stages so that neither of you is knocked out. It would be easier if you had another man to share the driving; you will of course observe the Sabbath as God's provision.

Well son, I could go on commenting till you are weary, but know that I am counting on the Lord to preserve you both in your daily movements. I shall be ever so thankful if aerogrammes are available, to have one whenever you have time to scribble a few lines. With much love to you both,

From
Dad

Belgrade
August 2nd

Dearest Dad

After writing the earlier lines we pulled out from the autoput rest-house for Belgrade about 8:30am. It was a scorching day and in fact the sun has burnt down on us all day long. We have been glad of the roof we had fitted, and have also been drinking gallons. We came to Belgrade without further incident, stopping at a tank station on the outskirts to find the address of the British Embassy. Without too much difficulty we came over the river and into the town. There are few of the old buildings left, but massive matchbox flats all around. There is not a lot of wheeled traffic in the town, though there are many people. We found the Embassy quite easily and soon had your two welcome letters.

The next place where we stopped was Topola. We admired

greatly the mausoleum of the Serbian Royal family. The mosaics have a wonderful colour and freshness. Most of the Gospel stories are illustrated on these beautiful walls. I took several slides of the mosaics but doubt they will come out.

We moved on from there for a few kilometres and have come to rest by the side of the road. The sun has set already, only 7:00pm. I have had a shower from our little portable shower. It has a bottle into which you put the water, a pump for building up the pressure and forcing the water out, and a length of hosing with an adjustable nozzle. I had a most refreshing cold shower on two litres of water. Monika also had a wash inside and has been doing odds and ends of washing. She is now getting the supper ready, which will be potato salad and some frankfurters bought in Belgrade. We spend less than 5/- a day on food and about £1 a day on petrol on average. We may get into Greece tomorrow, but I doubt it. Already we find our speed is cut down by the narrow winding roads and the journey ahead seems to stretch out a long way.

August 10th Turkey – Have run out of lightweight paper, so will have to continue on this, a relic of my stay at Borlands college. The exercise book was labelled "Inorganic Chemistry". I am truly thankful that those days are now past. Since writing we have made progress, in fact we are officially in Asia having crossed the Bosphorous last night.

The stay in Edirne was most interesting, especially for Monika. It was her first sight of full blown Moslem life. In the evening we took our courage in our hands, left the vehicles carefully locked up and went into Edirne. Monika was fascinated by the life of the bazaar and repelled by the filth of it all. Again we took our courage in our hands and had a meal in a restaurant. Monika had a good view of the kitchen and all the filthy things they did there, but was still able to tuck into the food. Actually cooked food is fairly safe, as are boiled drinks.

August 14th Laodicea – Rather a long gap to fill in! The ruins of Laodicea are a few miles outside the city on the way to Hierapolis; there are odd bits of carved stone and some remnants of buildings. Hierapolis is much more impressive, with a fairly well preserved aqueduct system, outdoor theatre and an old church. There are lovely limestone terraces and warm alkali springs. We decided to stay the night there and parked our van amongst the ruins. It proved to be a bad decision for we were eaten alive by sand flies. Monika developed an attack of diahorrhea and vomiting, which more or less kept us busy for the morning.

August 16th – We crossed the border into the upper part of Syria this morning.

August 20th Beirut – After typing the above lines things have not gone so well. First it became obvious that Monika was developing bacillary dysentery. Secondly, as we came to the Lebanese border we found the chassis of the caravan had broken. I thought at once of sending the caravan back to England. We camped that night just inside the Lebanese border wondering what to do. Next morning we started off very slowly towards Beirut and after five miles noticed a small welding shop. With some difficulty the old Moslem

Camping by a beach in Northern Greece, the last paved roads until Pakistan.

fellow was able to weld the broken chassis and seemed satisfied with
£2 and a tin of apricots.

The next morning we repacked the medical cases and crockery
so that we could send the three heaviest items by ship from Beirut
to Karachi. We drove into Beirut with the van and had it inspected
by a really most helpful Armenian. He assured us that the welding
was good, and nothing extra needed doing.

By the next morning it was plain that sulpha-guanidine, which
I started Monika on the night before, was not touching the bug so
we started on chloromycetin. This seems to have done the trick and
she is much better this morning.

Must close now and get this in the post.

Very much love to all
Monika and Howard

127 Karangahape Road
Auckland, N.Z.
August 16th 1962

Dearest Son

Tonight Mother is at the Ladies Fellowship meeting at the hall, acting as a "model" for a hat trimming competition, so I guess there
will be some mirth! She has also spent a busy day in town at the
mart, getting bits and pieces of furniture to set up her latest purchase of which she has just taken possession.

I was very interested to have an air letter from Colin this week,
still in Lahore awaiting a permit to enter India; it is a trial to be thus
kept in mid-air. Colin was interested to hear you are on the way,

and looks forward to seeing you on arrival – and to hear of the trials and deliverances experienced along the way. He mentioned that he had seen a Volkswagen with a 10ft caravan attached in Lahore, which looked as if it had just come out of the box. So he hopes that you find conditions much improved since his trip.

The long distances between the places you have given as wayside addresses, make it almost impossible to guess where you may be – last word was from Graz – so hope you received No's 30, 31, 32 & 33 sent to Belgrade; a duplicate of 33 was sent to Amman, where 34 & 35 also went, with duplicates of 34 & 35 to Teheran.

We are quite unable to guess how far along the road you may be, but day by day commit you to His keeping and trust you are learning more of His all sufficiency.

August 20th – Your wedding day! So this will carry a belated and loving greeting to you both. I hope you made it some kind of celebration. That was one of the recommendations of Mildred Cable when here, to help keep one from becoming stale and stodgy! I wish I knew just where you are; but it was quite an added joy to the remembrance of this day to have your interesting letter posted somewhere near Adrianople, Edirne today.

Mother left on Saturday to help with the cooking at Child Evangelism camp at Orewa (school holidays); but the appointed cook arrived on Sunday so she was home again about 11:00pm.

A card from John Bennet arrived today to ask your address in Britain, as they would like to see you before you leave!!

Much love from
Dad

Next to St. George's Cathedral
Jerusalem
August 26th 1962

Dearest Dad and Mum

I thought I would take the opportunity of an air- letter service to let you know that everything is going along quite happily. The day to day reports must sometimes sound as though we are enduring great hardships, but this is not the case.

The last letter must have come from Beirut when we were rather disturbed about the caravan. However there has been no further trouble in that direction, the welding seems to have been a good job. We have shipped to Karachi three of the heaviest items of baggage that we had with us in the caravan and this must have lightened our load by about half a ton.

Jerusalem is really a wonderful place and well worth spending a month or so just looking around and reading quietly. I'm sorry Dad that you didn't take the chance when you were going back to N. Z. The temperature is quite bearable, about 76 F at midday, with cool evenings. The traditional sites of the Nativity and Crucifixion are most unworthy and it is a pity the Israelis didn't blow them up with a bomb. The most interesting place we saw is controlled by Catholic nuns, the actual pavement where the soldiers mocked Christ, Herod's cistern for supplying his fortress and the arch where Pilate said "Behold the man".

After some talking to the Anglican authorities here, they agreed to allow us to park our caravan on their school playground. However, the agonising moment came when we got the caravan halfway through the gate of the school and then it stuck. At last a kind-hearted Muslim policeman came to our rescue and gathered several bystanders and we manhandled the caravan back out into the street – it had been blocking the traffic causing much confusion, as Arab traffic is not noted for patience. After we had got the caravan out our police friend showed us an empty site just opposite the cathedral, and on the edge of no-man's land. This has been a wonderful provision, for the police are always on duty and have been most friendly towards us.

Old city, Jerusalem.

We will move on today towards Amman and pick up our letter from the British Embassy. From there we will press on with all haste possible – 25 mph – across the desert towards Bagdad and the Persian border. I expect our old enemy the heat will really bite us as we go over the desert, but it will not be for too long as the mountains we will climb in Persia are quite high.

We look forward to hearing from you maybe in Teheran, or Kabul, then care of Robbie Orr in Multan, after that Colin.

With very much love from us both
Howard and Monika

Road from Amman to Baghdad, over desert.

127 Karangahape Road
Auckland, N.Z.
August 27th 1962

Dearest Monika

It is the queerest thing to be writing to you and Howard, without knowing just where you are, or whether the letter will ever reach you!

With the map I have tried to figure out just how far you have gone, and of course am glad to have Howard's travelogue which tells me where you were ten days ago. Today's from Beirut was most welcome; but I must confess that it looks a very long way from there to Bagdad, and even further from Bagdad to Teheran and then to Pakistan.

I am very sorry to hear that you had such a severe attack of bacterial dysentery and hope it does not occur again; I know it is part of the price of travelling in the east, but in your present state it is so much more distressing.

Then when I think of the heat, dust and weariness, and realise the burden the caravan must be, I hope that rather than jeopardise your own health and that of the little one, Howard would rather consider abandoning the caravan on the roadside and pressing on with just the Land Rover. Property and "things" are of no importance compared with YOU.

It would not be easy for you to part with Barbara, and the dear friends at Tubingen; the Lord grant that she may find true rest in Himself, and full provision for her every need in the daily pathway. How very lonely life can be for some.

Just yesterday I was reading a review of missionary work in Iran and was surprised to find that Teheran has almost two million of population. The Christian work was mentioned as being very small, though the Christian Missionary Society and Presbyterians have been there so long. The survey also mentioned the Presbyterian Hospital who allowed Colin & Gladys to park their caravan on their enclosure when they passed through.

We are longing to see you both, and will be so glad when the next few weeks are past.

With much love from
Dad

Amman Jordan
August 22nd 1962

Dearest Dad

The saga starts once again. After lunch we said goodbye to the kind Muslim policeman who had befriended us and kept an eye on our caravan during the time we were there. We headed back down the Jericho road and before long were at the Dead Sea. I had a swim there, Monika would not. The salinity is all that they say. I got some in my eyes and was glad to get out and have a long shower to wash it out. We pressed on over the Jordan about the place where Jesus was thought to have been baptised – a most lovely river and spot- and started climbing the hill towards Amman. We stopped by the side of the road, Oh what a hot night it was. We went on in the morning to Amman and were delighted to receive no less than four letters from you.

August 28th – We chugged along into the Syrian Desert. It was really hot. The road was good at first, but then began to get the most awful corrugations. After a few miles of this, I feared for the welding job. We did however manage to get to Rutba on the Syrian Border before noting that there was a crack. I edged along slowly, but about 50 km out of Rutba the chassis really broke in two places. We took the Land rover back to Rutba and for £10 they reluctantly agreed to bring a mobile welding unit out to the caravan. By 11 pm the job was done. We slept through until 6 am and got back on the road. Alas! After a further 70 km the whole thing broke down.

We are now in a very miserable position, about 250 or more km from Bagdad. The sun is blazing hot. We have transferred all the gear to the Land Rover and are contemplating leaving the caravan where she lies.

September 2nd, YMCA Bagdad – Shortly after the above was written we had a lunch of sauerkraut, neither of us could eat it. Monika felt sick with the heat and her nose began to bleed copiously. I had second thoughts about the caravan, figuring it was better to try to get one of the passing big lorries to loan me a tow rope, with which I somehow might be able to struggle into Bagdad. I stopped several trucks, but the heat was terrible and I did not blame them for wanting to go on. Later in the afternoon, when we had almost decided to abandon all, a convoy of five big tomato trucks from Amman came along. They stopped, and in no time had hitched the caravan up 3ft or so by the broken towing hook and chassis onto the back of their truck. We set off in fine style bowling along at 45mph with the caravan being smashed to bits behind the truck. They had already seriously damaged the front of the caravan trying to back, while they were getting it onto the road and off the desert. Still, they were goodhearted fellows trying to do their best to help us. We roared on through the night and arrived in Bagdad in the busiest time of the morning and had a most trying time in the traffic until the lorry drivers dumped us in front of the airport customs on a piece of waste ground. They had been most kind to us and asked for no money at all. We did however give them some cans of fish and tins of fruit, which certainly did not repay all the trouble they had gone to.

I was able to go straight away to see the British Consulate. He proved most helpful, advising us not only about the caravan, but also accommodation at a reasonable price at the YMCA. A most charming Assyrian Christian called Solomon John finally bought the caravan. After paying 25% duty on it I walked away in the end with £37.10. Better I suppose than leaving it in the desert but better still if we had never thought of bringing the thing, and listened to good advice.

We pressed on from Baghdad having been fortified with a good meal from our friend Solomon. By evening we reached the border with Iran, went through the Iraq customs and slept by the side of the car near the customs under the light of a beautiful starry sky. It was a little disturbed at times by howling dogs, but nobody came near us. We continued in the morning and were startled to hear that we just missed a massive earthquake that took place directly across the route we would have taken; 20,000 people perished in the earthquake. We thanked God for His deliverance. If there had been no trouble with the caravan we would have been in the middle of it.

September 6th Teheran – Monika went and collected your welcome six letters from the embassy. The home news was like cold water on a hot day! Meanwhile I had been out to the Land Rover place and had the oil seal on the right rear wheel renewed, and a thorough check of oil grease, tightening of the nuts etc. We just cannot afford to stay in Teheran, much as we would like to, a bed alone costs £2 a night. We have been into the Afghan question and have decided to go ahead via Afghanistan. Either route is bad. As the Land Rover chap said, "the roads are like hacksaw blades", but the Kabul route is about 500 miles shorter and there is no desert.

As you say, the strain of the journey is beginning to tell on us both. This morning I offered to Monika to fly her to Peshawar or Kabul, thus missing the rough road. She would not hear of it, and said she would be worried all the time. I trust we are doing the right thing.

Fondest love from us both,
Howard and Monika

A narrow escape from the severe earthquake in Iran.

127 Karangahape Road
Auckland, N.Z.
September 4th 1962

Dearest Howard & Monika

By the time this reaches you any difficulty caused you by the earthquake will be past, and we shall have news. Meantime you can understand how we have tried to work out where you may be, and what may be necessary for you to do.

Yesterday I went to the reference library and examined their "Times Atlas of the World", which is well detailed as to distance and also contour, and worked out step by step the stages to Lahore both via Quetta, and via Kabul.

The run to Baghdad looked fairly straightforward, and then it looked as if you may follow the road from Baghdad via Hamadan up to Teheran – right through the affected areas. So of course we have wondered whether you lingered in Baghdad and missed it, or pressed on and were at the centre of things. If you were on the western side of the 'quake, one can imagine how impassable the roads would be for some time.

From the maps it looked as if you could take an alternative route south to Basra, thence via Shiraz to Quetta. A map does not show the state of the roads, but it looked feasible.

Then it has occurred to us that if you are in the stricken area you may be caught up in relief work medically; anyhow it is all speculative, we do not know! As Blyth reminded me, you are both in the Lord's hands and He will care for you better than I could.

We were so pleased to have your air letter yesterday from Jerusalem and to know that you were both feeling better; of course we were amused at the refusal of the caravan to become part of the Anglican establishment and can picture the owner sweating a bit until the monster moved backwards! Whenever I see the big pie-cart being towed into Queen Street at night, I think, there goes Howard's caravan.

Mother has a few days relieving at primary school again, and is also happily busy with her "properties", one of which she has for sale.

Time to close now, so much love to you both from
Dad

Kabul
Sunday Sept. 16th 1962

Dearest Dad

Dusty, exhausted, our goods battered to pieces by the roads, Monika affected by the bad roads, me with a nasty bout of bacillary dysentery, yet triumphant in Christ, we have really arrived in Kabul.

So much has happened since I last wrote from Teheran. The day we finished typing the letter, we left Teheran and got onto the road again. That night we had our first experience of sleeping in a village hotel in a tiny mud village by the railway line. Early next morning it was so cold that sleep was no longer possible so we got up around 5:30 am and were soon onto the road to Mashad, but not before we were grossly overcharged by our hosts.

As we progressed the villages became smaller and smaller, finally it was just a barren desert with an occasional irrigated patch. Ah! The sky in Persia – no wonder they have such poets. The blue is incomparable and with the jagged mountains and wide spaces, it produces an almost unbelievable, Walt Disney type of effect. However, the condition of the road deteriorated, until it was really bad. The road became more sandy and full of treacherous potholes. With dusk falling we passed a rather dirty sort of inn and pressed on, the road becoming worse and worse. Eventually after 260 weary miles that day we stopped at a *caravan sarai* in the middle of the desert. It really was a most remarkable place, an enormous L-shaped room with raised sleeping places let into the walls, a central accommodation for the animals. It could easily have put up one hundred travellers. We were alone in one section of the large room in perfect safety. All went well until about 2:00 am when Monika started having severe abdominal pain. I was afraid that the roads had done their worst and passed the night in great fear and trepidation.

When the morning came she seemed little better. I kept her at rest for as long as possible but it was obviously impossible to stay. We journeyed out and got to a small village, at the edge of which was a building I thought may be a hotel. It turned out to be a police post. However, they were charming fellows and asked us to share their barracks with them. This worked quite well, as there were only two of them in a ten bed dormitory – the only trouble being that they slept on bare boards. Next morning they would take nothing from us for their kindness.

All through the next day, at an agonising 10 – 15mph we bumped our way to Nishapur, the closest railway station. I knew there was an American mission hospital in Mashad and was sure they would help us out. So, next morning I put Monika on the train to Mashad. I easily covered the 80 miles to Mashad, arriving three quarters of an hour before the train, as well as having a look at the grave of Omar Khayyam on the way.

Dr & Mrs Handwork put us up in their large bungalow. Dr. Handwork had some new tablets that were anti-uterine contraction agents, so glad to clutch at any straw we invested a few pounds in these. We left in the late afternoon for Herat, having spent a happy day and night at the mission hospital. I wish I could say that the work there is flourishing; it is not. I think this is largely due to frequent staff changes and the large new hospitals being erected in Mashad. The hospital was practically empty of patients.

The road to the frontier, (border of Iran and Afghanistan), was not bad at all, plenty of corrugations but few pot holes. We spent the night in another Persian "hotel". I want to forget that night. It was one of the dirtiest places we have been in, just packed, with people sleeping up to three in a bed, and really smelly.

The border crossing from Iran was a leisurely affair. As soon as we got into Afghanistan the really bad road began; just humanly impossible. We pressed on to Herat, which we reached as night was falling. So after the inevitable eggs for supper and a good sleep, we took Monika to the airport. It was with great relief that we found there was a seat to Kabul available and gladly paid the £11. The plane was a real old DC3, and taking off the pilot held it down on the runway for so long I wondered if it would ever get off.

I then headed south with all speed possible, down the first stretch of the new Russian built road that will connect Herat with Kandahar. The Americans are connecting Kandahar and Kabul. About forty hours after setting out from Herat, I at last arrived in Kabul. The local people had told us this journey would take us five days.

Meantime, Monika had arrived in Kabul and met with a wonderful Christian reception from Dr. & Mrs Christy Wilson, who pastor the united church here. They are wonderful people with a true love for the Lord and for the local people. They are not permitted to engage in direct evangelism but have widespread contacts among the people.

Monika had recovered quite well from her trip and tribulations and was quickly getting to know many of the vast community of American and German foreign women here in Kabul. I should think that for the size of the town, Kabul has more foreigners than any other place in the east. The Russians have a huge contingent about 2000 strong, and there are many hundreds of Yanks, as well as Germans. All are engaged in some sort of aid project or other. Kabul is a mean sort of place, Monika does not like it. It is dusty and built around a stone mountain. However the climate is wonderful, Pakistan has nothing to equal it.

We went to the morning service and had a good time listening to Christy preaching from the latter part of Romans 13. There were well over one hundred present, mainly Americans. Afterwards we stayed to lunch with the Wilsons.

September 17th, Kabul – We went and saw the local director of Medicare, an American benevolent institution which provides doctors for underdeveloped countries. During the course of conversation it became obvious that here was a real possibility for entering Afghanistan. He showed us over the 150 bed hospital that serves the whole of Afghanistan for elective and much of the emergency surgery. It was really pathetic to see the very sick people there; the dirt, flies, and stink were hard to bear.

We will move on to Peshawar tomorrow, and then will not spend much more time before getting on the road to Karachi and for home. Our money has held out well, despite all the emergencies and I think should see us home perhaps with £20 to "spare".

Kabul is certainly a disappointing place as a city, but one's heart goes out to the people. Poor as dirt, yet likeable people, who look you straight in the eye – then there are just hundreds and millions of nomadic tribes-people. There is no doubt of the weight of darkness here, and that spiritually it would be a much more difficult place to be in than Pakistan. Yet, it is much needier, and there is a terrific spirit of change; every year some new reform is carried through and there is slight liberalisation. Well, the Lord knows what is best for us, and we will be happy when we see just what this is.

With very much love
Howard and Monika

Pathans with camel loads of firewood, Southern Afghanistan.

118

36 Ferozepore Rd
Lahore
24th September 1962

Dearest Dad

Well, here we are at last!

It does not seem as though eight years have rolled by since I was last here. Once more the place is hot and sticky, just as it was when I left. Also the country around about is flooded, but not too badly.

What a joy to see Col and Gladys again! They are quite well, but are tired of waiting around for their permit to go to India. They have unofficial news that it is granted, but they will have to wait for official confirmation before they can leave for Calcutta.

They are living in very close quarters here in 36 Ferozepore Rd, and have been so for the last three months. We are camping with them, with Col and me sleeping on the veranda, and Monika and Gladys sleeping inside with the kids. We have had a pleasant two days with them, but are ready to move on to Multan tomorrow.

We rather hope we will be able to get to Karachi on Saturday and if all goes well take a plane on Sat. 29th, Sun. 30th or Oct 1st. It would take approx. twenty four hours to get to Sydney and then the N!Z! plane would get over to Auckland about 6 pm the same day. We will let you know by cable just which day we will be arriving, when we get down to Karachi.

Many thanks for your letters, also for Mum's letter. We are both well thank you, but it is much hotter here in Lahore. The car is still running well but bounces around a lot more now, since we have no load on board.

Will close now with very much love
Howard

Chapter 6
Back to Pakistan

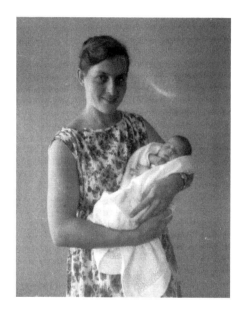

Monika with newborn, Naomi.

33 Ingalara Ave
Wahroonga
Australia
Tuesday February 1963

Dearest Dad

Well, we finally arrived yesterday with the minimum of trouble and difficulty. On the plane Naomi slept solidly for the four hours from Auckland to Sydney, apart from one feeding time. The plane was quite full, but only one other baby travelling.

Sydney is very hot and steamy. We were at Helen Ogden's place last night. I spoke on Romans chapter 8 to Helen's bible class for women of the district.

Baby is settling down a little better to the life of travel and is very hungry despite the heat. I was able to buy a book on ophthalmic surgery which seems to be very good.

Well Dad, I cannot thank you enough for all you have done for us during our stay in N.Z. Nobody could have been a better father to Blyth and I. I'm sorry that you have felt my failures at times. At least I cannot blame you for these things!

The sun is setting and Angelos (baby) is sounding as I write these words. Wahroonga is a lovely spot.

With v. much love,
Yours Howard

127 Karangahape Road
Auckland, New Zealand
February 21ˢᵗ 1963

Dearest Howard and Monika

Once again it is the queerest thing to be writing as I did in 1962, without knowing where you may be! Fortunately I feel less anxious now than I did then, knowing that with Naomi to care for, you are less likely to take her into places unsafe for you all.

This has been a queer week. Sunday, I spoke on Isaiah 6 at Wiremu St., after we had lunch at Ken Thompson's. Monday all day and Tuesday morning, I worked till I was weary at Milford, getting Ted's place spic and span, as he hopes to sell it. He has spent the week sorting out their possessions and deciding what to do with them, it is a harrowing business to break up home after the death of Lil, it makes the absence so keenly felt. Tuesday afternoon was a long committee meeting at B.T.I. (Bible Training Institute); then on Wednesday, Thursday and today I have been busy at the shop. Dick is having his holiday and Karangahape Rd. is having its special half yearly sale in which all participate. Special bargains draw the crowd and we have had a busy time.

I have not yet come to any conclusion about Dick's offer to buy the business. Blyth has been busy, so have I, but we may make time this weekend to talk it over.

Sunday – Blyth and I had a session together last evening, and have decided to accept Dick's offer in principle, details will need to be worked out. One feels it is the end of a chapter in life, leaving the final one to be written, and that one will need to plan the days carefully so that time is not frittered away. After 56 years in pharmacy, and before that 2 or 3 years on Saturdays from 8:30am to 9pm cleaning shop and running messages for a draper, I realize I had no education and no youth. Yet, the Lord has supplied every need, and the first reaction is one of relief that a change of activity is ahead.

Circulars from R. Grubb, Norfolk & Miss M. Barber N. Finchley were returned.

Much love to you all from
Dad

Christchurch Vicarage
Karachi, Pakistan
3rd March 1963

Dearest Dad

Well, praise the Lord! Here we are back on Pakistani soil once more. I last wrote from Sydney soon after arrival there, I believe. It was very hot in Sydney after Auckland and the first night Naomi slept very badly.

The flight onward from Sydney to Singapore was a very pleasant one. There were four people in the enormous BOAC 707, so we had plenty of attention.

We flew onto Calcutta 1 pm, arriving at Dum Dum airport 4:15 pm. Again, a long, weary drive into Calcutta by bus to find Colin and Mr. Smith (brethren from England) waiting for us with Mr. Smith's car. We piled in and were soon at Colin's new flat. This proved to be a rather nice, ground floor flat in a quiet Calcutta backwater. The weather was hot and sticky and the place was infested with mosquitoes. The windows were not adequately screened. Colin plans to get this done but I guess he is rather short of cash with the baby coming etc.

Both Col. and Gladys were in good spirits. Alastair and Verona are fine and healthy and developing very fast. Alastair speaks with a terrific Indian English accent!

Calcutta is a filthy place, rather like London. The air is full of grit and smog. Poor Col. I think already he wishes he were back in Pakistan.

We came on to Karachi yesterday and are hoping to clear the baggage we sent from Beirut through customs. Monika and Naomi will fly on to Taxilla, while I go by road. Our Land Rover is here in fair shape.

With much love
H. & M.

127 Karangahape Road
Auckland New Zealand
March 11th 1963

Dearest Son

After a cold spell for a few days it has turned warmer and except for a little wind it is a comfortable Sunday.

I need only to report that Mother's new address is No. 11 Wyoming Avenue, Murrays Bay. She has bought another house just one street down the hill from the Manin's, gathered everything here that belongs to her, and had the carrier remove the lot ten days ago. Of course I am not blind and could see things missing, though she said nothing about it. So on Friday morning as we were driving into town I just dropped the question, "Are you thinking of going to live at Rothesay Bay?" That brought up the old, old story.

My only reply was that in view of 1 Cor. 7:10&11, I could not think of consenting.

I am very conscious of my own failure over the years, and am desperately sorry that you boys have parents who have so shamed you. If nothing else, may our experience be a warning post to you. Thank God, I have Him for the rest of the journey. So far as I know my own soul, He has kept me from all lack of forgiveness and resentment. Unless mother has a new experience, she is likely to be a tragically lonely, old lady.

Len Goold has arrived home, and the assembly is giving him a welcome home on Tuesday evening. In spite of the most recent events at home, the brethren wish me to express the assembly's words of welcome. I'm not sure whether it is my own excessive sensitiveness, or the enemy's attempt to silence me. It is possible, if one is in correct adjustment with the Lord, to continue to serve the Lord through good report and through evil report, but it is not easy under the latter circumstance. The consistent continuance of

Blyth and Janette, their wedding day.

yourself & Monika and Blythe and Jan, is a continual cause for thanksgiving to me, and has saved me many times from being overwhelmed by discouragement.

Much love from
Dad

23rd March 1963

Dearest Dad

Many thanks for your recent letters, and all the news of home.

I am not surprised that Mum has shifted down to Murrays Bay. The district is so much more to her liking than Mt. Eden. I fear in some ways that I am to blame for this move. When she kept on about the "old, old story", in some exasperation I suggested to her it would be better if she went off on her own, and that you seemed to make each other very miserable. I am not so sure that this is the best answer, even in the short term, and certainly not for the long term. God has other plans than these for both of you, of this I am sure.

Well, the pangs of the initial settling in are now over. It is still very cold weather, thunder and rain having returned once more over the past two days. We have both now had a week of language study. My own study is going very slowly indeed, with only one hour per day. I have forgotten a good deal and was glad to start once more at the beginning. I hope to have worked through the book before going up to language school in Murree on May 6th. Monika has been getting on very well indeed. She has a good teacher who has nothing much else to do and so is able to spend a good deal of time preparing the lessons.

Howard at a threshing floor in Pakistan.

We went to our first meeting of the brethren in Rawalpindi yesterday afternoon. The singing was really wonderful, it is a long time
since I have heard such singing. One of the local brothers has a real
gift for composing hymns and my(!) how they sung, accompanied
by hand drum, hand organ and tambourines of various types.

The hospital work is certainly demanding of time. We start
operating at about 5:00am, sometimes 4:30am, depending on how
many patients there are. We do about 60 operations a morning,
mainly cataracts. I have been taking out an average of about two
a morning. I am slowly picking up skill, but it will be some time
before I would be happy to be left on my own with one. A visiting
American eye surgeon and his wife were here for three days this
week. He did some operating and was very bad compared with Dr
Christy, who is a beautiful surgeon- he has a wonderfully steady
hand, is quick, and very even tempered and kindly.

We are happy here, and every day learning some new thing.
Our baggage from England arrived during the week and I picked
it up from the station. It is mainly in good order, just a few things

broken. The three trunks from Beirut are still held up at the wharf. I hate to think how much they will cost by the time they decide to clear them. Baby is feeding better now after getting over her cold. I will finish the circular soon, I hope. I started it the other day.

With very much love
Your M. and H.

Christian Hospital, Taxilla
Pakistan
Thursday 7pm, April 1963

Dearest Dad

The day is almost spent. It was very pleasant but busy. The house is still beautifully cool, while the outside temperature is rising daily. I almost have everything in shape and order and I think it is the nicest home we have had. Yesterday in the bazaar I bought some very colourful curtain material for the kitchen windows, this is to stop people looking in.

The three pieces of luggage from Beirut are now making their way from Karachi so that in a few days we should have all our belongings. Not many things broken so far, but the china box is still to come.

This afternoon I washed my hair and sat in the back garden to dry it. There we have a water container with a tap which is intended for watering the garden, but one gets all sorts of surprises. Four men washed their feet there, others their hair or clothes. They are also using it for mixing mud which they are putting every year on the roof to make it rain proof.

Baby was not so well for a fortnight, she had a bad cold and is still a bit chesty.

The other day I went with Howard to a special meeting at 'Pindi, which the Assembly was having. How different it all seems at first, but I was thrilled to see them so eager for the Lord Jesus. We all sat on the stony floor of the building and courtyard, shoes off, men all close together in the front and women and children at the back.

I just wonder how you are on your own. I wished I could come and make the home nice for you. I have indeed prayed for this not to happen, but you know the word so well "All things work together for good to them that love God". Poor Mum, life is hardly worth living that way, but I must not judge.

Very much love
From Monika, Howard
and Naomi (she is sitting on my knee).

Chapter 7
Penetrating Central Asia

A minaret in Eastern Iran.

Herat
Afghanistan
October 1st 1964

Dearest Dad

This is written from a few miles outside of Herat, Afghanistan, on the beautiful new concrete road built by the Russians. I'm at a rest house, only just finished and again a fine building.

Well Dad, the trip is almost over and here I was going to write a daily diary! (Forgive the smudges. I am waiting for Jack Ringer to come back from Herat with a new radiator hose. Ours burnt out last night. The smudges are oil from my hands.)

To go back to the beginning… We left Bach Hospital on the Saturday at about 12:30pm and were in Kohat by 6:00 pm. On Monday we left for Peshawar and met Jack and Elma Ringer at the Afghan consulate. Visas were no trouble and we continued to the bank to collect our travelers' cheques. After clearing with the police we set off for Kabul. We arrived at Landi Kotal about 11:30 am and there met the two boys who were baptized two Sundays ago. We had prayer with them, and Jack gave them a word, and we had some simple food – a very happy and precious time of fellowship. About 2:00 pm we got to the frontier and drove on to Kabul.

We went around to the Community Church and met Rev. Irwin who is doing a locum for Dr. Christy Wilson (on furlough in USA for a year). He kindly agreed to look after the ladies while Jack and I took off for the North. We obtained a further pass for the North of Afghanistan and set off for Mazar-i-Sharif. We went through the beautiful and fertile Kabul valley on a good tar road. Around us were miles of apple orchards and vineyards, also delicious melons. At nightfall we were climbing the new road over the very high pass, only completed two weeks ago by the Russians. It is a wonderful piece of work with a long tunnel at the top; about 12,000ft up in the Hindu Kush range. Poor Jack has trouble with his ears and he could hardly hear for the next few days. After 100 miles of perfect road we bedded down for the night at a Central Asian *serai*. Jack made a great impression on the men with his Pushto (the main language here) and looked quite a sight seated on a bed surrounded by strong Central Asian faces.

Wednesday we set off for Mazar-i-Sharif. The good road stopped all at once and we were soon tossed about like a pea in a bottle. Before nightfall we had suffered two punctures. After a hard day's drive through mountainous country we arrived in Mazar-i-Sharif, the northern religious center. Here the main attraction is the shrine of Ali, fourth Caliph of Islam and a very famous figure. The shrine certainly is beautiful, I hope our slides of it come out.

We were soon on our way to Balkh, a city famous in ancient days, but now only a small bazaar with a few ruins. The road from here to Andkhoi, near the Russian border, was terrible. We pressed on over the bad roads to a place near to Herat. Here we slept in a small *serai* right alongside a nomad camp. All the next day (Saturday) we drove through land of the nomadic tribal people. They lived mostly in tents and yurts. What a mixture of people! We met Turkmen (very clever), Uzbeks, Pathans, Khirghizmen, Hazara and Mongolians, all sitting in the same teashop. Most were able to talk to Jack through Pushto. We really felt as though we were in Central Asia proper – the type of Central Asia that Mildred Cable and George Hunter knew. It was a real thrill to us. What peaceful lives these people had, no hurry or bustle here.

We were all set to drive from Herat to Kandahar and home, (Kabul), when the starter stuck. There was nothing for it but to take the Land Rover to a garage. They dismantled it and unstuck it, but now we are without a starter. We set out about 8 pm but had not gone far before we found the radiator boiling. It was then we discovered the leak in the pipe. I tried to patch it, but it leaked worse than ever. So Jack hitched a ride back to Herat to get a new pipe. I slept by the side of the road outside a rest house and slept very well. Now I am sitting waiting for Jack. It is already 10:15 am and so I am wondering if he has got mixed up with the police. We hope to reach Kandahar tonight and Kabul tomorrow and D.V. (God willing) return to Bach hospital on Tuesday.

With much love from us,
M, H, & N & ?

Howard at the Afghan rug weaving centre for the blind,
Herat, Afghanistan.

University College Hospital
Lahore, Pakistan
18/10/64

Dearest Dad

It seems as if we have moved into a different part of the world. The Punjabis and their way of life are certainly different from the northern regions, not so likeable. After a very weary all day's journey we arrived here late on last Tuesday evening with our luggage. Of course we had to bring everything, as we will need it, except the stacks of Howard's books and our beds which are stored at Bach Hospital.

Since this rough Afghanistan trip the car is not in very good order, especially the tires are causing much trouble. There is a good place here in Lahore where it can be checked over.

Tuesday we drove from the new hospital site to the old, not knowing where actually we were supposed to live. We spent the night with the Bavington's and moved into a very small apartment in the old hospital. It really is the smallest we have had, with two rooms, one kitchen and one bathroom. The bigger room is attached to the kitchen; we have divided it into an eating corner and the other half for sitting. The bedroom is quite small and besides a bed and Naomi's cot there is hardly room to pass to go into the bathroom. I have not yet found the answer as to in which corner to put our expected arrival.

The air circulation of this place is nil, so it will be very hot in the warm season. Even now we have mosquitoes and sleep under a fan.

Still, it could all be worse and in fact we are very happy here. Before I write more I must acknowledge your parcels, the first, the pot scourers which are very good, and the second, Naomi's clothing. But dearest Dad, what you send and a few things she has will be sufficient for this winter. We have all been keeping well. Hope to go to Multan for the delivery on the 26th.

Much love
Howard, Monika and Naomi XXX

Naomi's first steps.

127 Karangahape Road
Auckland New Zealand
October 27th 1964

Dearest Howard and Monika

When I returned from the Bible Training Institute this morning, there was a note in the door from the Post Office advising to call at

Balmoral office for a telegram from Lahore. Knowing that the trip to Multan was due on the 26th, I had been much burdened in prayer yesterday (26th) and the arrival of the telegram alerted me to the fact that things had not gone normally. Few prospective mothers would expect to go through all that Monika has faced this past month, when baby was almost due. And when I read 'all well' my first and lasting reaction, as expressed in my telegram is profound gratitude to God for His great mercy, for it is nothing less than mercy.

And of course I am pleased that in the providence of God, Naomi has a sister; if they are as good chums as Kevin and Craig, it will help to ease the unusual circumstances in which they live. The Lord bless them both and keep them in all their ways!

My guess is, of course, that after all the travel, the heavy work of packing at Bach and getting things into order, Monika was weary and the baby 'beat the pistol'. Among strangers, and with few at hand whom you know, I hope that you will make an effort to break the long day alone, if it is at all possible to look in even if only for five minutes. No mission has a right to expect its workers to be less than human to their folk.

For you, son, the next six months may be very testing at times; constant drive at hospital, not too much physical reserve after the summer, the need to take an active part in the home, the lack of time to be much with assembly activities will all tax you to the full. Yet God is able to make all grace abound.

Now it is time to run along to the prayer meeting; my night at Northbridge chapel has been changed to Wednesday this week, so they can have a baptism with some from Takapuna. Then on Sunday I'm due to give the final message at MSC house party. So far all I have in mind is "And Lord, what shall this man do?"

Much love to you all from
Dad

UCH
Lahore, W.Pakistan
29th Nov. 1964

Dearest Dad

We are all submerged with heavy colds at the moment. Monika has had a very light one, Naomi a real streamer, Faith has a high temperature, and mine also has been wet. The weather is changing quite a lot these days and winter is nearly on us. Sun is still warm however.

Work at the hospital is still very interesting; with Dr. Dunlap, one of the surgeons, away for a tour of Indian hospitals, this means more chance for surgery, and I am trying hard to take it with both hands.

We had quite a surprise during the week when one of the German brethren dropped in again. They were very keen for us to come to Kohat, starting next winter when the Herms go on furlough. I gave them no answer but told them we would think about it. My first reaction is that it would be good, but just as a stopgap until Afghanistan opened up. I don't know how you feel, but I wonder if the time for stopgaps is not finished. Surely the Lord will finally open the door to where He is leading us?

I have been wondering if it would not be possible to make a start in Afghanistan, just in order to get residence at first, as the honorary doctor to the small Christian school there. From this post we could settle down to learn the language and gradually get work among the Afghans. Of course I have no idea if either the government or the school would accept the idea. Please pray about this and tell me what you think.

How did your move go? I bet you must just be tired out. I wish we could have helped you out.

Must close now and try and finish these thank you letters.

Much love from us 4.
H.M. N & F

Naomi with Isam Din, our cook.

UCH
Lahore, W.Pakistan
28th March 1965

Dearest Dad

I hope that you received the cable we sent yesterday. The fact is that Monika has been very off colour for the past few days, with pain in her back and stomach and the feeling of being "blown up". She also has ulcers on her tongue which bother her a lot.

It seemed hard just to put a finger on the diagnosis, so I asked Dr Vick, a lady doctor, to have a look at her. Monika had a number of blood tests, stool test, x-ray done, but all came up negative. She got no better and became very worried about it all, so Dr Vick asked the opinion of Dr Dunlap (my boss). He felt a small lump in the lower side of the stomach which he felt was a granuloma. He advised operation, and after a time I agreed. The main thing was the state of mind of Monika; it was obvious that she would have no peace of mind until it had been cleared up what was wrong with her. She had all sorts of fanciful ideas, some of them including cancer and leukaemia. Some ass of a doctor in Germany had said she would not see the age of 25, and she is only a few weeks off this, his words have come back to her as a death knell.

Monika has had to have her milk stopped, so Faith is having a difficult time also getting used to the bottle all of a sudden. Naomi I have taken to my room, while Rose is looking after Faith. We will operate first thing tomorrow. I will assist at the operation and see exactly what the trouble is.

Well, it has come at a difficult time and all I can say is, "Lord, Thy will be done". He looks down in love and mercy upon us. He knows our hearts and how much we need His chastening and fresh lessons in following. It should, however, be me that am thus stricken and not Monika. Thanks for your two timely letters received tonight. I have read them to Monika and we have both appreciated the kindness and love of them at this time.

Monday 29th March – Dr Dunlap operated this morning at 8 am. The trouble is regional ileitis (Crohn's disease). The further outlook is not good, for this type of trouble tends to recur. However we will have to learn to live with it, if it does. Many thanks for your cable which came just after the operation. The verse was a particular help at such a time. Well at least we know where we are, and can just praise the Lord for His goodness. It will obviously mean a change of future plans, but just how I am not quite sure at the moment.

Much love from us all. H. M. N. & F.

Room No. 12
U.C.H.
The Lord's Day

Dearest Dad

It is exactly a week ago since I was admitted, but then I was in a different frame of mind, or rather out of my mind. My general condition and the thought of the two young children had so upset me that I have caused much trouble to Howard in what I said and how I acted. Finally, after fighting great spiritual battles with the evil one, the greatest ever in my life, I had peace. I had given up on life. Finally, the Lord's voice, "Be still and know that I am God… from whence cometh Thy help, not the hills, but the Lord…"

The operation went well and I knew nothing much for the next two days due to the pethidine and largactil. I knew it was no appendix, although they took it out at the same time. Now I know why I had no peace before, because I did not claim the precious blood of Christ, which keepeth us. Elma and I had talked a lot about it in Kabul, but here I had failed. Evil is very strong out here.

Howard will have given details of my illness and although I have recovered from the operation there is still a long way to go before I can do my duties. So far we can prove again the unfailing hand of the Lord in making provisions. First, this gift from Miss Downey and her letter, (as out of the grave), and then, the arrival of Rose Beckett back from England and her willingness to stay on in Lahore for a while. Howard sold the car, it is not finalized but most likely we hand it over next week. We shall be without transport, which will be very difficult, but the Lord may have a plan in this too.

Faith had to change overnight from breast to bottle and Rose had marvelous patience with her except the little one is crying a lot from a sore, raw bottom. My mouth is also full of ulcers so I know a bit of the discomfort.

Hospitals are great places for witness and already I had opportunities here. Yesterday to the 83 year old Franciscan father who had no assurance of salvation after 52 years of useless missionary work in Pakistan.

Dearest Dad, don't worry, the Lord is very near to us and you.

Much love
Monika

8 Currie Avenue
Auckland S.3 New Zealand
April 5th 1965

My dearest Son

I have been distressed for you both, and have scarcely known what to write, words are so feeble and one is so far away and can do nothing to help in the emergency.

I feel deeply for Monika; the subconscious carry-over from the unguarded prognosis of the doctor years ago, the pain now with the uncertainty of its cause, her thoughts for the children if she were to be ill, the approach of your exam, the preparations for removal to Murree would all press in on her consciously or unconsciously.

And for you, the grief of seeing your own suffer, the pressure of immediate circumstances, the uncertainty of plans for the future, and the accompanying heart-searching, have all driven me to the Lord again and again for you both. There is no easy solution to a situation like this; one has to learn to go THROUGH the storm with the Lord, and to trust Him in the dark. He does not propose to make stoics of us, and it may be normal experience to have an aching heart whilst trusting Him to work all together for good. Some of the mysteries of suffering will not be unraveled until the path here is ended. "What I do thou knowest not now, but thou shalt know hereafter."

My mind runs to a psychosomatic cause for the inflammation, with the realization that so far as she is concerned, it may be entirely unconscious. Looking back, son, the past five years have been filled with stress and tension far beyond normal; there were those lonely months in Parfrey St. when you were at Ipswich, the loss of the little one, the overland journey with its 'moments'; the time in N.Z. with its solitary days and broken nights at Panmure, the first experience with Naomi and so little understanding from Mother; and in the two years in Pakistan, long wearisome journeys, no settled living space, packing and unpacking, yourself and two babes to care for, and your own uncertainty, as to guidance, to share. It is all cumulative and I firmly believe that under such circumstances mother- nature may rebel and strike back through the body to secure relief for the psyche. We too easily think of infections and the body machine, forgetting that it is only a house for the tenant.

I think I can sense your own disappointment that cherished plans may need to be set aside, yet He who knows your steadfast desire to serve Him may be using this set of circumstances to put you in the place where He wants you to make Him known. Mileage may be the product of a restless nature and have nothing to do with the call of God. For the sake of your effectiveness in service, and for the sake of Monika and the children, I hope that if she is spared to you, you may be given a piece of work to do in one place until furlough time. The periodical uprooting every four or five years for a missionary family is unsettling enough.

I'm not jawing you son, my heart aches for you and Monika.

Auntie Flo has given me £5 for you, with her love and prayers. She is getting frail now.

Much love from
Dad

Dad with his Austin car, outside his last unit in Hillsboro, Auckland.

Chapter 8
Entering the Land

*Looking down the steep pass into
the Kabul Gorge.*

New Colony, Kohat
Pakistan
"Lord's Day"
Sept. 6th 1965

Dearest Dad

Greetings from Kohat, Pakistan! On Wednesday the 1st, the actual move took place. Albrecht Hauser came the previous night to Murree, where it had been getting daily cooler, to bring us into an oven down here. It's 37°C indoors and has been heating up again since our arrival. The Lord undertook wonderfully and all went well.

The first day we ate our meals next door at the Hauser's so that we could get things straight. Howard was sad to see that a certain insect had a marvelous time among his books, which were stored here, and had to dispose of a number.

We sleep outside, except Faith, who strangely objects, also to the mosquito nets.

I am feeling a little better and still think the slippery elm is partly doing the soothing work. I pray that I might get better as there are lots of activities going on in the assembly and I ought to take my share. Kohat is a very bad place for sickness and poor Howard is already down with dysentery.

Tomorrow he is off to Peshawar to arrange his visa into Afghanistan. He shall leave here on Tuesday for two weeks. He had a favorable letter from Medico inviting him to work in their hospital and asking the Afghan government for a residence visa. We shall see what the Lord wants; it's foolish to run ahead of His time.

Kohat is terrible just now for buying food, no vegetables and eggs. This morning seven eggs were bad out of twelve. Tomorrow I shall start language hours.

We are concerned for Janette and plead with the Lord. Next time will write more.

Lovingly, your roasted chickens,
Monika

In Kohat, with Faith and Naomi.

C/o Dr. J. Christy
Wilson
American Embassy
Kabul, Afghanistan
Friday Sept. 9th 1965

Dearest Dad

Here we are once more in Afghanistan! I'm beginning to lose count of the number of times we have been here, but looking back it must be the fourth time in the past three years.

On the Monday I went into Peshawar with the idea of getting

the ticket for Kabul and clearance for the plane flight the next day. I spent a very hot morning getting tax clearance etc. only to find when I came back at midday, that all the flights had been suddenly cancelled an hour before. I heard that the Indians had made an attack at three points on Lahore.*

I put out of my mind for the moment my trip to Afghanistan and my only thought was to get back to Kohat. I found that the Hauser's were already in a great flap. Mrs. Hauser was just worried stiff about it all, and Albrecht was also quite ready to quit. However, I hung on for a couple of days to see how things developed in the war. Where we were in Kohat was quite close to a rather large airfield. This was a hive of activity, with planes coming and going twenty four hours of the day. I understand that they were bringing dead bodies from the front, and there were plenty of those, and also prisoners of war.

Only once did we hear the sound of what could have been bombs dropping. However, this was enough to make me see that the war was a serious thing and was going to get worse before it got better. I decided to leave the next day by bus for Afghanistan.

We were almost the only people on board to start with. There were many stops, as you might guess, and we went very slowly the first miles to the Pakistan border. On the Afghan side the bus was stopped by ragged looking police every few miles to check for smuggling. They didn't find anything, though I am sure there was smuggling going on by the driver, but they would have to have been smarter to catch him.

We arrived in Kabul about 9 pm and had a warm welcome from the Wilsons. I will go off to Bost on Monday as planned and do

---

* The Indo-Pakistani war of 1965 was a culmination of skirmishes that took place between April 1965 and September 1965. This conflict became known as the Second Kashmir War, fought by India and Pakistan over the disputed region of Kashmir. On September 6th 1965 India crossed the International border on the western front making an official beginning of the war.

my medical work there. Monika will stay here with the kids, who will benefit from the cooler climate. Then, D.V. we will go back to Kohat in ten days if things have quieted down a little. If not, we will just sit here.

With very much love from us all, hope you have not been worrying about us.

Howard

Kabul,
Sunday 26th September 1965

Dearest Dad

The events of the past two weeks have just rushed by, leaving me panting for breath and waiting for my spirit to catch up with my body! My first medical work in Afghanistan is now a thing of the past. I thank the Lord for the way He has led us in these difficult days. It was surely the very best that could have happened.

I spent nearly two weeks in Bost, at their newly American built and fully equipped hospital. It was quite an experience. During four days I saw over 1000 patients and did about 140 eye operations as well as a considerable number of general operations, some of them quite big operations, such a prostatectomy and caesarean section. I also did refractions and sold a lot of glasses, mainly to the officials. The Americans working there were extremely low spirited but were encouraged by the visit. Bost is purely American built and is their project in Afghanistan. I have a warm welcome to return there and will do so on October 11th.

Monika has also been helping in Kabul, reaching the lives of some of the American ladies. It has been somewhat of a strain for her continually living in another's home.

Tomorrow I go the Minister of Health to discuss eye work in the Helmand Valley. It seems things are really opening up, but I will write again about this.

We are all well, and trust you received our earlier letters, and have not been too worried about things here.

Much love from us all
Your Howard

Afghan carpet woven in Herat.

8 Currie Avenue
Hillsborough, Auckland
October 10th 1965

Dearest Howard and Monika

Letters from Lahore and the other containing the bank slip both arrived during the week so have brought me up to date with what has happened since you left Murree. I think I sent six letters during

September, so their non-arrival indicates the extent to which mail is delayed. Both of yours were marked as "passed by censor".

Though I thought you were in Kohat at the time of the bombing, I did not feel concerned for you, expecting that the Lord would care for you all, and knowing that He kept Monika through much greater dangers during the war time. It concerns me much more that you should be in the place of His appointing and in the centre of the circle of His will.

I'm so glad that you all enjoyed the change in Kabul and the American food! What it must cost to have things brought across like that. I had an idea of sending a mixed parcel of bits and pieces in time for Christmas but with the visit and possibility of moving to Afghanistan, there is no knowing what your address will be by then.

Janette has been very poorly since Friday. Developed acute pain in the chest, symptoms seemed to me to be acute pleurisy, which Dr. Adams has also suggested. Morphia injection made her vomit, pethidine has had no effect on the pain and just made her groggy, codeine was useless; she has had most relief with very hot water bags, and over the weekend Dr. Wilson has her taking achromycin, as she has had a persistent cough; says definitely not angina this time.

On Tuesday I will see the Bank about sending a draft for the remainder of the permit for this year – to Hammersmith as usual. When I know the amount, I'll give you details as to whose gifts included.

Yes, Mother has bought an £8000 house opposite Westlake Boys School. I saw it as I passed on the way to Manin's. Blyth does not think it looks worth it, but says it is nice inside. He thinks she will be out of it inside 12 months!

Much love to you all
From Dad

New Colony
Kohat, West Pakistan
Friday 22ⁿᵈ October 1965

Dearest Dad

Thank you for so many letters, which seem to be arriving daily. Yes, it is wonderful how the Lord always is a present help in times of trouble. As we were out of Pakistan and in Afghanistan we have not really experienced any danger or need. Miss Wrona (a deaconess) and the Pakistani brethren and sisters say they would never want to have missed the time during the war; it was a time of prayer, fellowship and blessing for all.

Since last month, when we returned from Afghanistan, Howard has only been at home for barely two days. As soon as he returned it was his turn to go to Lahore. There Heinrich Becht pleaded that he should get his family back from Kabul, as he could not get permission to leave the country. Having returned the family safely to Lahore, Howard had to get another visa for his second trip to Bost.

Since last Thursday we have been expecting him back from Afghanistan daily. He sent two telegrams telling us of a delay. Yesterday was supposed to be his return but so far no sight of him. People here are getting very restless about this and I hope in the future he'll show more concern for his present work here. There may of course be perfectly acceptable reasons for his delay; he may have met Colin in Kabul on his way home, or the Ministry of Health may not have given an earlier interview. I have a strong feeling he has arrived with this morning's plane and should be here for lunch.

The children and I have kept fairly well, although there is an awful lot of sickness due to weather change; malaria, flu and typhoid mainly. I have kept very busy these days, as Isam has so far not returned. This means at least three hours daily in the kitchen, two hours language study a day and massive preparations for Sunday School and women's meetings. I am really grateful for the opportunities, although I need to slow down again.

Nowadays we have to be very careful going out, as there is a terrific hatred of foreigners, and especially missionaries. Received slippery elm again, but there was no coffee in the package. Dad, here are some hints for Xmas. Would appreciate some warm "tights" I think they call them (woolen pants and stockings in one) for Naomi and warm vests if available. Where we are, one gets only necessities. Paper is gone.

Much love from us here, Monika.

Bamian (Central Afghanistan)
Sunday October 17th 1965

Dearest Dad

I am writing this from Central Afghanistan, from Bamian, a famous tourist spot here. They have two very large Buddhas carved out of the rock cliffs, and very interesting old caves. I hope to be in Pakistan on Tuesday and will post this letter from there, as I believe the postal service there is much quicker.

I think I last wrote a week ago. I stayed with John Hankins for the night last Saturday and then was off on Sunday afternoon for Bost. The plane was a DC3 and the trip was the bumpiest I have experienced. I felt sick but fortunately managed to hold onto my lunch, which was more than most of the others were able to do. I was driven down at once in an American aid vehicle the 90 miles to Bost and arrived about 7pm feeling rather ill. I had an early night and the next day was not too hectic. I saw about 50 patients and did one plastic operation – very time consuming. Next day was much busier with a great rush of patients from far and near.

I came back to Kabul on Friday, and on Saturday morning saw the Minister of Health, Dr. A. Please pray for this man, so far he has shown considerable cooperation. He asked us, (the secretary of Care Medico, who runs the Bost work was also with me), to undertake eye clinics from a mobile-type hospital at several centers in Western Afghanistan. I also put to him the proposal for an Eye Bank in Kabul, together with a small eye hospital and a training school for blind children. He promised to consider this and asked me to submit the proposal in writing. Please pray about this also, at last it seems that some solid substantial work seems to be opening up, after all these years of constant moving.

I was due to catch the Saturday plane back to Peshawar, but to my dismay I found that I had left my passport in Bost. They radioed down and it will be brought up by Dr. Phillips, an American surgeon who has been over here for a month's visit. I am very sorry about this apparent waste of four days, but wonder if the time has really been wasted or not. I came to Bamian and have enjoyed the little break in this beautiful place. There is no doubt I have been pushing things too hard lately and it has been good to have this time away from constantly meeting people. I feel sorry for the work in Kohat though and wonder whether it would be more honest to move right into Afghanistan. Our work seems to be increasingly here.

Dearest Dad, I am sorry to hear that you have been lonely. Despite your tiredness I still feel you would feel at home with us for some lengthy period. Feel free, Dad, to come whenever you are ready – we will always be ready.

With fondest love,
Howard and Monika.

Leper house in Bamian, isolated from village.

Enormous statues of Buddha in Bamian.

157

A war party of Nooristanis seeking to recover stolen sheep and cattle.

New Colony
Kohat
6th Jan. 1966

Dearest Dad

Although the year has well started, a very Happy New Year to you! May it bring you peace, health, joy and a little bit of comfort. For us it began very quietly. Howard was away in Lahore for perhaps his last visit to U.C.H. and has since returned to Afghanistan. He came home two days before Xmas, which was nice and I was very thankful as Naomi was just taking ill with pleurisy.

Over Xmas she was quite ill and also has no recollection of her birthday, but thankful to say she responded well to the penicillin injections and now is well on her way to recovery. Faith and I also got a nasty cold. I am still deaf with it.

The first thing we shall have to report in this New Year looks like a change of address. Howard may have kept you informed of the openings in Afghanistan and that it would be best if we moved.

158

Although nothing has been finalized yet, this is what he at present is hoping to do.

I have always been somewhat of a pessimist and nothing would surprise me. Sometimes of course, in the Lord's work one has to be the other way and Howard has very much that leaning. I will be rather sad to leave Kohat so soon and go over to Afghanistan in the middle of winter, with everything snowed in. Also to leave all the good opportunities for witness, which really for the first time I have had and enjoyed. No doubt if this is the Lord's doing He will provide even better opportunities for the future.

My prayer is for myself is that I may be filled with a new love that will speak to a new type of people. LOVE is the only thing one needs here, and to ask for it again and again, because soon after you come out one finds hundreds of things, habits which naturally would produce the opposite reaction towards them. But that God loves us as we are and were, and gave his beloved Son, is what one tends to forget quickly.

Howard ordered some very necessary furniture in Peshawar; so far we have always looked after stuff from other missionaries. Just a table, 6 chairs, desk, food-safe, a nest of small tables, bedside tables, two chest of draws, and two bookshelves, all for over 3000 Rs. It really knocks me over, but in Afghanistan these items would be double and everyone gets theirs made over here. We will also have to cook on electricity, (and buy a stove), as kerosene oil is imported from Pakistan and is exactly four times the price. I don't know how we shall find the means to live over there, but this must be the Lord's worry. One has to be indeed very sure of His guidance before one would ever undertake such an expensive step. So far He has met all our needs and His faithfulness is forever the same. Dearest Dad I don't want to depress you with all of this, because we keep still rejoicing.

Much love, Monika, Naomi and Faith

Faith and Monika drinking Coca Cola.

8 Currie Avenue,
Hillsborough
Auckland, N.Z.
Jan. 12ᵗʰ 1966

My dearest Monika

The mystery of the missing mail is solved at last! I was disturbed that no mail at all was coming to Currie Avenue, so last Friday I posted a circular to myself; when three days passed and it was not delivered I realized it was time to inquire at the post office. When I went to Rotorua in November, I put in a stop delivery notice. On my return I sent a commence notice and for two or three weeks received mail as usual. Evidently a new postman picked up the old stop notice and thought it still applied, so things have been piling up at Mt. Roskill Postmen's Branch. When I called there were 30 to 40 letters, Christmas cards, magazines etc to collect.

Among them, one from you on Dec. 19th, one from Howard at Kohat when Naomi was ill on Dec. 26th and another from Kabul on January 4th. So at last I am beginning to get up to-date on the news.

What an anxious time you had with Naomi! No doubt the Lord over-ruled in that Howard was at home at the time of her illness, after his long absence. I don't know how he would feel if he had come home to find she was in heaven. In the early days of C.I.M., (China Inland Mission), when there was so little that could be done for pneumonia, missionaries in western China lost one child after another in the very cold weather. He will not need me to remind him that she will be extra susceptible for some time to come, nor that it would be unwise to be away again for more than a few days until the winter is past. I have little doubt that the strain of the journey from Britain left its mark prenatally and has affected her constitution. "Old wives tales" her father will say! Very well, but he will find a little extra fatherly care may make a difference to her childhood!

Writing from Dr. Christy W.'s place, Howard tells of the negotiation for a house to live in and I think of all the work you will have to get ready for the removal, just when it is so cold for you all. I am surprised he was so thoughtless as to travel without an overcoat; once around the world should cure one of that mistake.

I really should reply to his air-letter along with this, but I am very tired, and have no light at all on the many expensive and hurried plans he is proposing. I can but pray for you all continually, as I do, and trust He will have you in His keeping.

Now to bed!

Fondest love, from Dad

Kabul
Thursday 27th January

Dearest Dad

This is the first note I am able to send from Kabul. The Lord has really brought us here safely and His hand was over us all the way.

The last few days in Kohat were hectic, and several good-byes I still have to say by letter. Last Thursday Howard went to Peshawar to arrange for a truck to take all our belongings from Kohat, including our furniture from Peshawar which was in the process of being made. This is the first time we have our own things.

Dr. Christy Wilson kindly took me and the children in his private car, he was on business in Pakistan, and Howard rode in the lorry. We kept pretty well together all the way. There was no delay of any kind on either border, for which we praise the Lord. It could have been very different.

Afghan border, crossing over from Kohat to Kabul with family, and possessions in the lorry.

We went straight over to our new house and the truck was unloaded ready to return. We just got the beds in order and went to sleep; it was 11:30 pm. Since then almost everything has been straightened and unpacked, only the light bulbs need changing.

The welcome here was terrific. Last Tuesday night about thirty people turned up at our place to give us a welcome party. Every family brought a box of food stuff and tinned foods, so we have a stock for some time. I never had so much food stored in the whole of my life. Everyday has been busy with people dropping in trying to be helpful.

It's still much colder than Kohat, snow on the mountains around about and in the back garden. Heating is a real problem and our arrangement is not good yet, also for cooking. We really need an electric stove, which costs £100 to buy. The children are well and getting used to the new surroundings.

Much love
Monika

Chapter 9
The Work

*An eye camp in full swing, patients waiting
to be seen post-op.*

PO Box 1503
Teheran, Iran
(This is the address for mailing
confidential letters to)
3rd Feb 1966

Dearest Dad

I am taking advantage of the travelling of Dr. Mortenson of the Team mission to send out this letter to you. I do not know when you will receive it. It does often seem that you are hearing our news from others first!

Well, these are wonderful days. The Lord has done great things for us, whereof we are glad! To start with the most recent events:

We had the meetings of the representatives from the different mission groups here in Kabul, Afghanistan, starting January 31st. What impresses me is the way the Lord worked to bring agreement. To one who has known the tensions and suspicions of missions in Pakistan, to see them all sit down and actually agree about something, was a sort of modern day miracle. I can testify that all the men from these missions are born again evangelical Christians. It was a joy to sit down with them for these days and have fellowship together.

My own position was a little difficult. I carefully outlined the position of the NZ assemblies, and it was interesting to see just how much they were willing to change the constitution and byelaws to accommodate the assemblies. For instance, right through the minutes they changed churches and missions to more neutral words; they dropped the word denomination and made membership on an individual basis instead of a mission basis. They also strengthened the clause on the basis of faith being in the inspiration of the Scripture, and added the clause concerning the atonement and salvation through faith.

The first two officers of the Mission are, as you see, executive secretary, Dr. Christy Wilson – a wonderful man of God whom the Lord has prepared for this work for many years. It has been a precious privilege to have fellowship with him, he has just done everything for us to get us into the country, even down to giving us all the firewood etc. that we needed during our first days here. The other officer of the Mission, strange to say, is me. I am not sure why they chose me, nor of my qualifications to be Treasurer, the title of "Spender" would have been better. My knowledge in book-keeping is hazy, but apparently this is one of the key offices in the mission and carries with it a major responsibility for planning and carrying out the policies of the mission.

I am not sure I will keep this office permanently as it is difficult to say what will happen when the first Board of Managers meeting takes place in the summer. What it does mean is a wonderful demonstration of confidence, by the other mission groups, in one they can hardly know, and who has frankly told them of his abiding connection with the assemblies. I trust that those at home will not feel too shocked at all this, and that on the contrary, the Lord will send those of His choice from the assemblies in NZ to take part in the work here.

I can hear the bell ringing at the front door, so will close with very much love. We are all fairly well, the weather has been cold but not freezing as it usually is. We still have no good heating arrangement.

Yours
Howard

Kabul in the winter, showing the Kabul Wall, built in the 12th Century by Buddhists to keep the Muslims out.

8 Currie Avenue
Hillsborough
Auckland S.3
February 13th 1966

Dearest Son

In hope that this may come per Mr. T. Haughey to Kabul, I am making a few comments I may not send through the mail. You may know Mr. Haughey, (one of the big architects here), is in Tamaki

168

assembly, and is NZ chairman of BMMF council; Mrs. Haughey is daughter of Dr. Pettit and older sister of Mrs. Murray Fountain.

Your letter regarding the Mission conference in Kabul and the minutes and constitution sent to Mr. Goold came through in about four days from Geneva – in marked contrast to your local mail which I suspect goes missing a good deal.

I'm so glad the conference was harmonious and purposeful. One can scarcely think of a more suitable executive secretary, he has such wide acceptance and has already done so much for Christians visiting the city; he will be also well known to local authority.

The appointment of a treasurer is a great compliment to you; professional standing may have something to do with it. Until money comes in more freely it may not involve a great deal, but having been a treasurer at Eden Hall and for WEC, I know how terribly time-consuming the job is and the concern for finances it engenders, especially when funds are short. You will need great discretion and to know when you are attempting too much. If it cuts across your medical work too much you will need to decide which is the most effective. Possibly you may pass the job on at the annual meeting; the more the work is spread the better.

I have also mentioned to Monika the trial you may both face in being among the European community as a 'poor relation' with neither the desire, or the financial ability to participate in the empty social life of the embassy and business group, and sometimes of church missionaries and their wives. Under those circumstances, and as your house is not near the city, Monika could well have to undergo a good deal of loneliness. You have your work and constant running about and seeing many people to occupy you, and may not realize what it means to her; in Kohat she had company close at hand and the opportunity of sharing in the work. You will be in the limelight (so appealing to the flesh); she will be at home with the constant care of the children and trying to make one shilling do the work of two. You will need to be very watchful. In reading George Morrison of Glasgow, on the life of Abraham, I noticed his remark that when Satan attacks an Englishman it is very often through his home.

Feb. 15th – The circulars have gone out to the assembly folk, and I now think I'll post the rest before they go out of date. Have enclosed a copy of the circular so you will know what went out; a reference to 'secret service' would have been dangerous. No doubt you will burn both this and the circular when read.

Much love to you all, from
Dad

PO Box 0
Kabul, Afghanistan
9th Feb 66

Dearest Dad,

I am taking the chance of Mr. Ostrander, local chief of Care Medico, going on leave to write you this censor free letter.

The last few days Kabul has been rather like England at this time of year, cloudy with a good deal of rain, and cool weather, though not actually freezing. This week has seen a few notable events, mainly the getting down to work on Kabul Persian, quite a different language from the Iranian Persian. The written language is the same but the pronunciation is different. Kabul Persian bears roughly the relationship to Iranian Persian, as Cockney English does to BBC English. Just as the Cockney, they drop their "h's" and add them "hon" again where they didn't "hought" to be.

We now have the loan of a car until we can get one of our own. This is necessary here, as we are right on the outskirts of town and public transport is in the very early stages. Gas is still quite cheap, being a government monopoly. Diesel fuel is a third cheaper than this and is the cheapest form of heating for the house. We have a diesel heater which we brought for £10 secondhand. It is now installed and at last is working satisfactorily. This of course only heats two rooms, but it also takes the chill off the rest of the house.

Another good development is that Care Medico has shown a good interest in supporting the eye project. It is a sort of quid pro quo for what I have been able to do for them, I guess. We may be able to get quite a large amount of aid from them in due course. It will be in the form of material rather than cash, and will be approved project by project.

I called the Ministry of Health again today, but was told to please call again on Saturday morning – he was seeing the Ministry of Planning today apparently. Thus I am no further ahead with the signing of the agreement. I think it will be a red enough letter day to send you a cable when the agreement is finally signed, even if it does cost nearly 2/- per word!

Well, I will close now, as Monika would like to draw a plan of the house on the back. Really the views here are wonderful, and with our spare rooms here, there is no further reason why you and Uncle Ted should not come here for a stay.

Very much love from
H.M. N. & F.

PO Box 0,
Kabul, Afghanistan
8th April 1966

Dearest Dad

Fifty seven was the number that we had been waiting for. It was visit no. 57, when at last the Minister of Health signed the eye project.* The big day came on Wednesday April 6th. I had the whole proposal retyped during the afternoon after consultation with Christy Wilson. We eventually changed some vital words over the authority issue, which left authority fair and square in our hands. I took it to the Ministry of Health at 9 am and found a very warm, cordial atmosphere. They agreed without hesitation to the important change that Christy and I had made, and at about 9:20 am I signed with Dr Aziz S., (Director General of Health).

Immediately afterwards, I went and started work at the hospital. The first patient I saw was the Minister of Finance who needed spectacles. We then saw a string of patients and I did the first two operations.

Well, it was the end of a very long process and of course the beginning of another equally long process, but we trust many years longer.

Dr Albrecht H., the head of Care Medico is here at the moment and has expressed great interest in the eye project. It is at such times I would like to have your advice, for I find it rather perplexing to know how far to go with some of these things. Of course the whole

---

* The Eye Care Agreement was the basis for the eye camp work that would be carried out in many remote parts of Afghanistan, the establishment of a blind school, relief work carried out in flood and famine situations, and the foundation of NOOR Eye Hospital in Kabul.

Signing of the first Eye Care Agreement.

eye project will cost a great deal of money, just how much I would not like to think! So far we have this interest from Care Medico and an enquiry from Germany. We will now have to get working on raising all the finance required.

We have cabled Dr. Jock A. telling him that the project is signed and to come urgently. Dr. Alec B. will be coming from Peshawar with Pauline and his two little girls very soon. We have no nurses in view as yet for the work but have written to one or two. Of course we are very much hoping John S. will come for the post of pharmacist and that Colin might come for the post of business manager; that about completes our list of possibilities.

We all seem fairly well. I am under a certain amount of tension as the program gets under way, but of course basically very thrilled to be here and to have such worthwhile work.

With very much love, yours
Howard

Dr. Christy Wilson and friends.

Kabul
20th April 66

Dearest Dad

It has been a long time since I wrote, but we just have been very busy or rather our house has. It's a real stopping place for everybody, especially folks from Pakistan. Of course we cannot keep up running a guest house and trying to do something more constructive.

Howard has so much on hand. The work here in the hospital is growing, besides he still has obligations to other places; Bost, Jalalabad and a new avenue has opened towards the north for an eye-camp, Kundus. We very much wish that Dr. Alec B. would come sooner to share in this work.

The work among the blind is also growing rapidly. It is about time a real school for the blind was established, run by an experienced teacher of the blind from abroad. Volunteer workers, Christians of course, are doing their best. I am one of them, trying to keep them

Rosemary, at the bazaar.

supplied with books which I type from Persian into Braille. This is for thirty boys, who now come regularly. We had to limit the numbers. The only Afghan girl who was teaching them was married the other day and left for India to take a nine month course in a blind school there. You may remember this couple in prayer as they are foundation members of "His bride" here on earth. The little boy from next door is still coming daily, and there has been some opposition from his father because of a chorus he learned here.

The garden is just lovely now; cherry and almond blossom, tulips, lilac and irises. Your seeds in the boxes are coming out and also other vegetables I had sown.

I heard that Jan is to have another operation. She really is brave and how the Lord blessed her.

Very much love from us all,
Monika XXXXX

Two men from the blind school reading Braille.

PO Box 0 Kabul
9th June 1966

Dearest Dad

It was good to get your letter number 34, with the enclosures from the treasury. First of all, we did receive the Waltham draft and I trust by now you have received the acknowledgement for it. It is possible to send Bank of England notes by registered mail, there is certainly no restriction here as there was in Pakistan. There is also no reason why good parcels should not be sent, as you remember we have duty free status here, so it would cost us nothing to receive them, although they would certainly cost a lot to send. With reference to the question of censorship in Afghanistan, this certainly exists, although not on a regular basis. Any special news should still be sent via our friend Dr. Johnson.

Well, this has been a busy time for us. I seem to have been keeping up with the strict essentials of living, and lately have even been cutting off before breakfast. Work no doubt seems to increase relentlessly as the days go by. It will be a pleasant change to once more sit down with the books and study for the D.O., (Diploma in Ophthalmology), instead of the continual pressure here. You are right in saying we are standing up to it fairly well. This is because at last we have found our niche. The security this gives is wonderful, especially after being tossed from pillar to post for years.

I wish you could have been here recently. Herr W. from Germany, the head of a blind mission, came through. It was rather a fiasco at first, as he arrived with no one to meet him, (we received his telegram telling of his arrival on the day he left Afghanistan). After this initial setback, relations improved quickly. He was obviously impressed with the setup here and the possibilities, so much so that he offered to undertake the support of Monika as a start.

This mission has been working for fifty years among blind people in Iran, and thus you can see has been prepared for cooperation here. They apparently have the money, while we have the workers and the projects to spend it on. The amount they want to put into the work was staggering, no less than $60,000 annually, this is apart from support for Monika. This would certainly be plenty to run our work here. It is indeed wonderful and reminds one of the word, "Before they call, I will answer". This does not of course lessen our links with the NZ brethren. It is not because I do not trust the blind mission but simply because my roots are so well down in NZ. Yet even as I say this I wonder when we will see the fair shores of NZ again?

Well Dad, we would still love to see you and Uncle Ted at anytime, but of course will not press you to try something you feel unable to do.

With much love, Howard

Chapter 10
The Labour

Kabul airport, Ariana Afghan Airlines DC6 – fires were lit under the engines to get them started.

8 Derwent Drive
Purley, England
8th January 1967

Dearest Dad

On the move again! This time I'm heading for Dublin.

The weeks in England have slipped by and here we are facing the Diploma of Ophthalmology exams!! It is hard for me to believe and as always, I feel unprepared. The exams start tomorrow morning 10 am with a viva. Anatomy and Physiology in the afternoon, (I can't get away from it!), and then each day there is another paper or viva until Thursday, when I guess we will know our results.

Monika is coming up to the last week or so of her pregnancy and unfortunately developed a heavy cold after Christmas. Faith originally started off with the cold and we have all had it except for Naomi. The weather at the moment is very cold with snow falling all day up at Purley, (England). The snow has frozen solid and is quite slippery but it does not seem to have delayed the planes to Ireland.

Well, I will close now – still another thirty minutes to wait before takeoff. Amazing mercy and grace!

With all my love
Your Howard

8 Derwent Drive
Purley, England
15th January 1967

Dearest Dad

We got there at last, from a good and happy disposition (isn't that what Naomi means?) to Faith and then to Joy. Now you have three grandsons and granddaughters.

It was quite a surprise for Howard when he returned Thursday midnight from Ireland to be greeted by a nearly twenty four hour old Joy. On Wednesday morning he telephoned but everything was still alright, I put the receiver down and was on my way to the kitchen when my waters broke.

The mid-wife was the nicest person I could have hoped for, my own age, very competent, quiet and helpful in every way. She came at 12:20 am Thursday to the house and Joy was born twenty minutes later, at 12:40am. All went very well and without complications. She was 7lbs and has lots of black hair, it will no doubt get fairer.

Tomorrow we shall hear about the exam results from Ireland, in the morning post.

Could you please let Jan and Blyth have this news. I just wrote to them the day before she was born.

Love
Monika

8 Currie Avenue
Hillsborough
Auckland NZ
22ⁿᵈ January 1967

Dearest Howard and Monika

Your telegram and air-letter from Monika are indeed great cause for thanksgiving and praise to the Lord. First the Dublin results are so much to be grateful for, and secure the purpose for which you are in Britain. I was noticing this week on our prescriptions that three of the ophthalmologists practicing here have F.R.C.S. but no indication of other exams. Maybe that is just a swank!

And we were most interested to hear the details of Joy's arrival. We had no idea that the NZ procedure would not be followed – doctor and obstetric hospital, and are so glad of the way things worked out.

Both Blyth and Howard were born in the house. Howard came early while Nurse Firth was on holiday, but we had Nurse Christensen staying with us. I woke at midnight to find Esther leaning over the bed with Howard in her two hands, and the umbilical cord looped around his neck, in danger of choking. I quickly called the nurse from the next room, and she took over. A narrow shave, my boy! Mother had not wakened me when her short labor commenced, she wanted to dodge having Dr. Isaac stand around watching, as he and the nurse had done for Blyth.

The weather is miserably cold in Britain, but will it be possible for you both to relax a little for a fortnight or so before taking up the work in Kabul?

Much love
Howard

Howard and friends at Tekuiti home.

8 Derwent Drive
Purley, England
12ᵗʰ February 1967

Dearest Dad

Well, this may be our last letter for the present from England, though I would like to get out a circular before we finally leave these shores.

Ahead there lies another time of testing as we seek to put the eye care proposal into effect. Curiously, I am not worried about the Afghans, but have some vague forebodings about some of the other folk in the mission. It does seem there has been a good deal of reticence from Kabul of late, and the original team spirit seems to be rather fragile at present. Why, is rather hard to say. Perhaps the reason is that most doctors are prima donnas. It is embarrassing really to know what to do with people who openly seek position, and again this is a problem quite beyond me. It is at times like these that you well realize what J.O. Saunders and the others must have faced when he was made General Director. Spiritual principles are not at stake, but fellowship is involved. I ask myself if I should step aside from leadership of the mission? Am I as free from the desire for power and glory as I think I am? However, there are a few binding promises, the main one being to the Afghan government to stay with the work for at least ten years, though this does not of course mean that I should always be in charge of it. You must have come against this same rivalry many times during your years on mission committees. Well, well, it is hardly fair to talk about forebodings at this stage when the Lord has done so wondrously. We will just have to trust Him for each step of the way and now especially for relationships. I know that this will be increasingly one of the crucial things for us.

We are planning to fly back to Kabul next week.

I have just been outside with Naomi and Faith, tossing up the rubber ball on the lawn. It is still frosty here, but a lovely day. We thank the Lord for this place.

Much love from us all,

Yours
Howard

> PO Box 0
> Kabul, Afghanistan
> 20th May 1967

Dearest Dad

On return from Herat yesterday I read your letters with interest including up to no.29.

I often thought of you whilst I was there and meant to get down to writing a letter, but was always pushed for time. Most days we worked from 8:30am to 9:30pm with a break for lunch.

Sorry the circular that I wrote as soon as we arrived back, has gone astray, I enclose another with this letter.

"…Five hundred hands reach out, with voices crying, 'Doctor sahib, look at my eyes.' or 'Look at my baby's eyes'. The baby begins to scream, nurses try to keep order amongst the noisy throng. Is this what Jesus experienced when the crowd pressed upon Him for healing? The scene is the ancient city of Herat, former center of the Nestorian church. Since the dark days when the Mongol hordes extinguished civilization and all life in that area, Herat has been a center for Islam.

Four of us – two nurses, a pharmacist and I set up our first eye camp in this city, where 80% of the people suffer from eye diseases, principally trachoma. After an interview with the Governor and Head Doctor we started work in the two hospitals of this town. In the Women's hospital we were so thronged at times it was difficult to draw breath. At the end of our stay we had seen over 2000 patients and done 327 operations.

The more significant thing, to us, was that for the first time in many centuries four believers met together to remember the Lord in the breaking of bread and each person we operated on was commended to the Lord Jesus Christ for His blessing and salvation.

In February we left England with some regret, and on arrival at snow clad Kabul it was good to meet old friends at the airport, including the Afghan doctors and Dr. Alec B. who had ably carried on the work in my absence.

The folk at the Ministry of Health were, of course, interested to know when we would start on the erection of the buildings for the blind institute and hospital. I was glad to be able to tell them of the OXFAM gift, a generous gift sufficient to build the blind institute.

*A large crowd of patients waiting to be seen
in Herat.*

Our eye program is called "*NOOR*", which means light. It is the word used in the Urdu and Persian translations of the Bible when Jesus said," I am the Light of the World". Under this program we are permitted to bring in eye doctors, nurses, teachers, an optician, office workers, builders, a chemist, and we have vacancies for most of these tasks. We look forward to Dr. Jock A. and his family joining us; he is a fine ophthalmologist with wide experience in Pakistan.

Recently here in Kabul, a handful of us sat on an Afghan rug with an open Bible and a tape recorder in lieu of a hymn book, to supply hymns in Persian. An hour flashed by in deep fellowship, prayer and a word from the Lord. Insignificant, yet observed by the Beloved and owned by Him. We praise Him that He is doing a work in the hearts of many at this time, in this land. More than this we may not say at present; we are still very much the church in the catacombs. All I can say is that the fellowship is sweet.

Daily, except Saturdays and Sundays, we have a class in the afternoon in our house to study Persian. We are getting to the stage where we can lead simple conversations and also have started to read the Scriptures. The progress would have been faster but with three little girls around there is never a dull moment…"

Well Dad, I certainly have a few thank you letters to write, praise the Lord for them however, His goodness has been unfailing.

Weather is heating up now and it is hot enough at night to use one blanket. I expect the opposite is happening in Auckland.

With all our love
Howard

8 Currie Avenue
Hillsborough
Auckland NZ
28th May 1967

Dearest Howard and Monika

You are so constantly in my thoughts that I did not realize until I looked at my notebook, that it is nine days since I sent No.31! When this comes I trust the Herat job is finished and you are together again at home.

I have mentioned before that Ted was still complaining of continued severe pain and had seen three or four doctors since being in England. This morning Blyth received a 'phone call from Mrs. Ross at Portsmouth to say he has been put in Southampton Public Hospital and had an operation for tumour on the spine, which revealed extensive cancer. There is no likelihood that he will return to New Zealand.

It raises the question as to whether it would be any comfort to him for me to go over by air, and this evening after tea Blyth is putting in a person to person call to the surgeon who operated. Mrs. Ross said the doctor insisted that he is not to be told of his condition, and that poses a problem for me. Yesterday Ted sent a telegram which I received an hour ago, "In hospital, progressing satisfactorily, writing, Ted".

So much may have happened before you receive this!
Dad

Monika and new arrival Joy, Naomi and Faith behind.

Kabul Airport
4th October 1967

Dearest Dad

I am sitting in the restaurant redeeming the time. We are forlornly awaiting a packet of eyes (for corneal transplants), which did not come in on the jet this morning.

Dad, sorry that you did not come here on your way back from England, but glad to know you will now be safe at home and in your own little place recovering from the past weary months. Dear Uncle Ted, he found a faithful friend who stood by him to the end. He himself fought a good fight and finished his course with joy. Well done, good and faithful servant!

I am off to Herat tomorrow with Prof. Barrie J. and Dr. R. We will be there on Saturday for one day of trachoma surgery before they go on to Teheran and then onwards to London. Their visit has been a busy one, with not a spare moment. We saw King Zahir Shah for two hours on Tuesday evening, and will see him again tonight. He has bad eyes. We have also seen a large number of people who could be helped with corneal grafting work.

Sorry to say, Joy has been ill for the last four days, vomiting everything she takes down. I won't leave Kabul until I feel happy about her situation. Monika has had a rough time with it all.

With all our love
Your Howard

*King Zahir Shah and officials coming out of
his palace.*

PO Box 0, Kabul
5th May 1968

Dearest Dad

Well, another busy time is over! The annual mission board meetings
finished on Friday.

It has been a time of intense and weary meetings for most, but
glad to say they spared me too much involvement in them. I was
called up to see if I had any ideas how to lighten the burden of our
executive officer, who has lately been overloaded with work. They
wanted to introduce some sort of executive secretary under him.
This seems to me a poor principle and in my opinion the authority
should rather be spread over a larger number of men. Again there
was reference to some "executive", who would coordinate the medical work. There was in fact a lot of woolly thinking. To my surprise
there were no kick backs about the building work or lack of plans.
No doubt they are used to these endless delays and failure to fulfill
promises. There seemed a willingness to look around their agencies
to find some money for the building projects. On our project a

number of new people were accepted. I tried hard to pry Dr. Novel C. loose from Taxilla but they would only agree to his coming over on short term visits, at least for the first year.

Tom Haughey has written suggesting that he ship over from New Zealand a wooden building frame for the blind school and that Graham Craig come over and put it up for us.

All I can say is that all these rather intense committee meetings make your head reel. I still don't know how you were able to cheerfully put so much time into them. One helpful thing that came out of it all is that it seems likely my function in the mission will become less, and wide areas of detailed work will be handed over to different ones. The phrase "kicked upstairs" is not exactly appropriate, but almost!

Well must close now and get to sleep. Love from all, as ever.

Yours
Howard

PO Box 0, Kabul
24th June 1968

Dearest Dad

I should be sleeping but I am waiting for Howard to return from the Murree conference. I have prayed that he may be refreshed and rested. He really has too much on his plate but as you keep mentioning, it is partly because things are not organized. If only Howard would start one day to plan his day and stick to it as far as circumstances allow, it would be a beginning. It's not at all in him and I could smack myself for keeping on nagging at him about getting things organized. It is very hard for me to help, as he does not communicate his thoughts very easily. I am praying and wondering in which way I could be of some help.

We had a visit here from a Jordanian brother. He spoke several times at the Kabul Community Church and we had personal sweet fellowship together. I am longing for such dear brothers and sisters in Christ in this country.

The days are warm now and humid, this is because of the rains in Pakistan. With us is a German brother. I had such a shock when he said he came to stay for a month. He has only one arm, poor soul and needs lots of looking after. He came to take photos of the blind work. I think he was disappointed not to find the new school built yet.

I am frequently reading this verse of a prayer:

"I would not ask for pleasant ease,
Nor even with gladsome tasks that please
The fleeting hours employ,
But in Thy presence may I know
What'ere my lot, where'ere I go,
The fullness of Thy joy."

We are all fine.

All our love
Monika

PO Box 0, Kabul
29th June 1968

Dearest Dad

It looks as though I am off on my travels again! I can see you sigh
with the weariness of it all, but I still quite enjoy these trips. I am
travelling on "company" business of course, in fact taking the application for finances for the hospital, on to Bonn. I hope to leave on
July 4th but we shall see if I actually get off then or not.

I had a good time of quiet and prayer during the Murree days
and walked a good deal all over the hill. I walked up the path where
in 1954 I felt the call to take up medical work, and this time felt
that I should take the advice of J.O.Saunders, to step down from

my position in the mission. You are right; the bold initiative to start something is not perhaps what is needed to carry it on. I am completely happy to serve, as well as to lead. I came into this without ambition, no doubt from time to time I have been proud of what I have done, but I can honestly say that the main stream of my thought and life has not been that of grasping after power and position. It has always seemed to be an ignoble thing to seek and unsatisfying when you get it.

The other point I raised with J.O.Saunders, was one which has troubled me for some time, the increasing red tape of the mission. I am left with the uncomfortable feeling that the committee system can be manipulated by unspiritual men to get their own ends. I am slowly learning the ropes of managing committees, but am curiously more unimpressed the more I get into it.

Well must close now. Our one armed brother is still here, a perfect pest whom I wish we could shift on.

Love from us all,

Yours
Howard

8 Currie Avenue
Hillsborough
Auckland NZ
30th June 1968

Dearest Howard and Monika

I think the last gift I reported was 18 dollars from Morrinsville assembly. July 1st brings the beginning of the third quarter for which

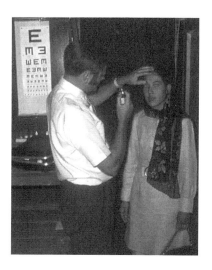

Howard checking patient.

the Bank permit is issued, so I'll go into town this week and arrange the transfer. It has been a lean quarter and there is only 143 dollars toward the 300 needed. I hope you will be able to write something for a circular this month to let friends here know of matters for praise and prayer.

Of course I did not see the TV report on the outgoing building material for the blind school and the young NZ doctor in Afghanistan, but several mentioned it to me, including the lady in the flat next door. They tell me the material was photographed on the wharf, so I expect it will be shipped out soon if not already on the way.

We expect Gladys Blair and the children to arrive here on the 14th.

As you said, committees may be used by self-seeking and ambitious men to get their own way; in the long run that kind of work does not prosper. If the committee consists of men who want the will of God, His Spirit does guide them, and their unity in the Spirit is strength. In both the China Inland Mission, (C.I.M.), and the Bible Training Institute board, over the twenty years I was in them, I cannot recall a dispute or contention; difficulties, yes and differences of opinion, but without acrimony. The first thing that struck me when I attended C.I.M council meetings was whenever a difficult matter came up, a halt was made for prayer and the difficulty was solved. In both bodies, council meetings commenced with unhurried prayer of everyone present.

Now I think I'll away to bed; I have been weary and depressed this week- probably because as usual July is dark, cold and wet; my mother died in July, in July my Dad took ill and died in early August and last July Ted was in hospital; memories come rolling back and tax the frame that is wearing out. How thankful I am to have memorized some portions of the Word. Wakening in the night, I go through some of the Psalms. I wish I had memorized more, it is not so easy to break fresh ground now.

Much love to you all, from Dad

PO Box 0, Kabul
25th July 1968

Dearest Dad

I am now expecting Howard back from Germany any day, possibly on Saturday. Although he has so much on his mind he has continually remembered us here with postcards for the girls etc.

From Howard's letters I understand his trip has been rather disappointing and the job of raising money is not nearly complete.

He feels exhausted travelling from place to place and longs to be back again. Unfortunately, when he gets back he is going to have the whole burden of the work. Dr. Alec B. is taking every nurse and competent doctor with him on the eye camp to Bamian. I am disappointed because I thought he was more considerate. But we must look to the Lord for daily strength and keep on loving the brethren.

Colin and Gladys, and others including a nurse and a blind school teacher, will all be arriving for NOOR. Howard needs much strength these days as all these new people coming means finding new homes, getting visas to stay etc.

I am teaching the blind girls four days a week. It is very enjoyable but I am flat out afterwards, my reserves are not what they used to be.

Very much love from us all
Monika

Blind work extends to include girls.

PO Box 0, Kabul
22nd November 1968

Dearest Dad

The days are slipping quickly by and soon we will be with you again! I can hardly believe it, it still seems to be a sort of dream.

I believe, in answer to prayer, the Trust agreement with the government will be finalized in the next few days. We will then get into action and lay the foundation stone for the blind school and start building, and also the hospital. I seem to have lived with this project for the past three years and it has become quite a burden in some ways. It has been an illuminating exercise in the fact that whopping mistakes can be made by those who should know better, including me! I suppose it is the only hospital I will ever build.

We won't be sorry to get away for a time. The pressure of personal conflict has been bearing down on us and we feel the uncomfortable feeling that we are at times the target for it. It is the ones who work around the back door and seek other ways to express their disagreement that cause some heart burning. I had felt that I was immune to this, but lately have sometimes found myself angry, a sure sign that we need to get away for a break and a change of occupation. I think the heavy study program for the F.R.C.S. (Fellowship of the Royal College of Surgeons) will be the ideal alternative to the years of mental and physical activity I have put in recently. I am certainly making up for the lost years of boyhood and then the A.G.S. (Auckland Grammar School). There is hardly a day goes by but that I have to exercise my limited capacity for creative thinking to the full. I often wonder "why me?" but since Dr. J. has not shown any great capability to oversee a thing and think it through, it has resolved the question as to whether I should at this time lay aside the leadership of the work. I will think it over again when we return (D.V.) to Afghanistan later next year.

Colin is keen for me to make a contact trip through NZ, meeting all the "worthwhile" people, but honestly I don't have the real energy to do it. However, maybe I should get Blyth to map out a six to eight week program of meetings.

I hope it will not be too much of a burden for us to be with you in your house. Sorry we won't make it for Christmas, but it is just not possible this time.

Much love from us all,
Howard

Chapter 11
The Furlough

*Monika, one of the speakers at a Ladies Conference, in
Christchurch, New Zealand.*

Address until May
260 Pettit's Lane North
Romford, Essex
England
January 1970

Dear Praying Friends

I am sorry that the year has passed without my setting pen to paper to let you know of our news and prayer requests. However, during the past months in New Zealand we have been able to see some of you face to face, and that has been better than a circular! We thank all of you who have prayed, given and shared your homes with us during furlough.

After six years away from home, we set off from Kabul by air to Auckland in January 1969. On the surface everything appeared quiet in the work we left behind in Afghanistan, but within a couple of weeks of our leaving a great deal of trouble broke out. Satan made a determined effort to silence the witness through internal disunity amongst the foreign workers of the mission. It seemed for a time as if the whole work might collapse. About this time we received a generous legacy from my Uncle Ted Harper, and after a great deal of prayer I decided to use it to make a short visit back to Afghanistan to try and sort things out. I went in the month of May.

It certainly proved to be the right thing to do, but it was heart-rending to see the havoc that had been wrought amongst sincere believers by personality differences. A start was made towards getting things on a right footing, but there remains a good deal to be done before the unity of the Spirit is restored. Despite the work of Satan amongst the foreign workers, the Holy Spirit was at work amongst the local believers, and while in Kabul I had the joy of meeting around the Lord's table with six who have since been baptized. Thus the Body of Christ in Afghanistan is being established and built up.

Good progress is being made with the building of the Institute for the Blind; the Government requested that its first use be as a temporary eye hospital until the medical block is erected.

The time at home was much appreciated by us all. We enjoyed seeing our family circle as well as being once again at our home assembly. A highlight for Monika was her baptism at Wiremu St. She had thought to take this step with the first of the believers on the field, but felt she should wait no longer.

I spent time during the year in study, first at the Bible Training Institute until Easter, and then studying for the primary Fellowship of the Royal College of Surgeons (F.R.C.S.). Unfortunately I did not pass this exam – only 21% of the entrants passed. I'm now planning to re-sit the exam in Britain.

As I write, we are nearing Panama on our way to England. In November I was offered a position as ship's surgeon on the Empire Star. So we sailed from Napier on December 13th to the hearty farewells of dear friends there. The voyage has been relaxing and something of a holiday after our busy year.

Monika had an unfortunate accident when she went out on the passenger deck late one evening for fresh air, just outside the door she startled a large sleeping sea bird which hissed at her. In stepping backwards to avoid it, she tripped over the high doorstep, hurting her leg and twisting her ankle badly. I have put it in plaster and hope there is no bone injury and will have it x-rayed at Panama.

When we arrive in England, about January 18th, we will go to the address above, a missionary home. Until May I will be continuing my efforts to pass the elusive F.R.C.S. I am also hoping to accept the generous offer from Professor Barrie Jones of Moorfields Eye Hospital to take an unpaid post on the professorial unit. It will give me further operating experience under first class supervision such as I could not get on the field. This will take us up until May when we trust, D.V., to set our faces once more toward Kabul.

The past year has been difficult, as it well may have been for many of you. As we have held on quietly and prayerfully, waiting for the Lord to work, He has given us the words "Be still and know that I am God" and "No man having put his hand to the plough and turning back is fit for the kingdom of God." They are good words for us all to take into the unknown year ahead!

With cordial greetings
Yours in our Lord Jesus
Howard and Monika Harper

"The Empire Star"
December 30th 1969

Dearest Dad,

We are approaching the harbor of Balboa (Panama) and the sun is rising. It really is good seeing fresh green again. The pilot came on board with a health officer and the tug boats are waiting to push us into place. We are here until evening, for the ship to take on oil and water.

Four of the crew and I went to see the naval doctor. The x-ray place was terribly antique, but we had good news, my ankle is only sprained.

Late afternoon we made our passage through the Panama canal, it was like going down a river, just enough room for another ship to pass us. The five locks through which we passed were most beautifully illuminated.

December 31ˢᵗ – We left the calm of the Panama waters and almost immediately found ourselves in rough seas. A big New Year's buffet was prepared but I did not feel like eating much. I went to bed with the children and the rocking motion soon sent me to dreamland. I found it too hard to review all the sad parts of 1969, so I only thanked our heavenly Father for all He has sent us, both of joy and sadness.

January 5ᵗʰ – The sky is dark, the sea is grey and English winter has come. A very strong wind is blowing onto our sides, bringing splashes of water right over our windows up top. There was a lifeboat drill but the boats were not moved for fear they could not get them back. We had another fire on board. My verse for today is "Have faith in God".

January 6ᵗʰ – What a night and day followed! Howard always wanted to experience a storm – he shall not forget this one soon. It started in the mid afternoon. When we went down for our supper, tables and chairs were secured and the sides of the tables were put up to stop things from sliding off. I did not feel like food but forced myself to eat. Things got worse. I didn't sleep a wink all night. Joy's cot kept tipping, doors slammed and downstairs there was a continuous sound of broken china, pots and pans. It was a job to keep in bed. Howard went to check on the children and the door shut on three of his fingers.

January 8th – We did not go far yesterday due to the wind and two fires. The hurricane, "Colorado", overtook us and is now forty miles ahead.

January 9th – The sea is like mountains raging, and you can hear the breakers roaring. We are caught in the gale. Does He care for a little ship tossed by the sea? He does. The lower quarters are all flooded and water is sweeping through the passage in front of the dining room and lounge. This is no time of enjoyment. Howard gets no study done.

January 13th – 350 miles to go. In fact, no one is sure of our position. There is no sun, moon or radar to go by and no reply from the radio. The sea looks almost black with dark clouds overhead. The swell is high but we are not rocking so much.

January 15th – During the early morning we reached Dunkirk. I was awake and watched from the deck. It was cold and had been raining. Remember in N.Z. they loaded the wool, two or four bails at a time. Here, they unload 12 bails in one go.

January 21st – We are anchored twenty miles outside of Hull waiting for the 2 pm tide to take us in. We reached England only a week late. The Lord was good to all, He supplied all our needs. We are in good health. After the customs come on board we will see if any trains run through to London, or try and hire a van. What a load of luggage.

How are you all? Much love from the five sea birds.

Monika and co.

The Empire Star in the Atlantic, huge waves,
a storm on the way.

8 Currie Avenue
Hillsborough
Auckland 4, N.Z.
January 18ᵗʰ 1970

Dearest Monika

You will know that you have been continually in my thoughts through the painful days on board ship, and the handicap of having to go ashore and get up to Romford with handicapped limbs. Truly your experience of 1969 was "here we suffer grief and pain"; you will both think of your first furlough as a time of trial and testing; I had so much hoped it would be an experience of rest and renewal.

Looking back over the time, it seemed to pass so quickly, though

207

to you both it may have dragged; so many of the things I wanted to say were unsaid, and I think of all that I meant to do and didn't! I was just beginning to know the children when it was time to leave.

It was good of you to write such a diary of shipboard-life, the first half of which you sent from Panama, we all enjoyed it and were glad to hear that the children were well catered for. I guess they will have nicer recollections of their first sea voyage than you.

BBC tells us of the very cold weather you are having, and of the heavy mortality through influenza. I hope there is some comfort in the house or flat you have, and that there is warmth and friendship in the assembly. I am also thinking much of Howard and the exam (FRCS) on the 26th – 28th, and so hope he is able to be in Glasgow a couple of days before the exam so that he is fresh.

Our fine weather continues, not quite so hot this morning, 72° with light cloud and breeze. Folks are returning from holidays and I expect this morning's meeting will be nearer normal size. I'm still doing the mailing list, maybe after the renewal cards come in, it will be a good deal smaller; in which case I think it would be well to send a letter more often.

I forgot to say Auntie Flo. gave me ten dollars for Howard and you. If you did not get mail from me at Dunkirk, please make an enquiry for it, I sent enclosures which Howard should have, I think they included letters from Serampore and Kabul.

Much love, from Dad

260 Pettits Lane Nth
Romford Essex
5th Feb 1970

Dearest Dad

Since that brief talk from Ayr, I have hardly had time to think. The shock of passing the Primary F.R.C.S. was so great that I have not yet adjusted to it. It also meant making a vigorous effort on the Moorfield front in order to establish a base of operations for the assault on the Final fellowship.

I came back home from Glasgow on Friday night, very weary, but I went straight into London Monday, to see Barrie Jones. True to his word, he has given me the post as research Registrar which he will make official, and I will get one paid session per week as outpatients officer to Hammersmith Hospital. I also start a two week Final fellowship course on Monday and the teaching at Moorfields is superb. I only hope I keep fit enough to handle this heavy program.

Fondest love, Yours Howard

8 Currie Avenue
Hillsborough
Auckland 4, N.Z.
February 8th 1970

Dearest Howard & Monika

"Sunday morn has come again, with its joy and cheer" but we never hear Uncle Tomcat and his kittens these days, they are scattered as far away as Romford and who knows where else. Instead we are listening to "Hymns for Sunday morning" and have just had a fine rendering of "O Thou who camest from above".

Quite a number of folk have phoned to congratulate you on the Glasgow exam. It is indeed a milestone and I hope the time in Moorfields will put you in order for the final. Have you any idea of the date when you will sit?

Feb. 11th – Sorry this is dragging its feet; it is very warm again, maybe I'll do better when the weather is cool. I was ever so glad to have yours of the 5th today with its news of things in Glasgow; as the postmark is London W.1 am I right in guessing you are staying at Bedford Place during the week? Do you get home for weekends?

It is a sacrifice for Monika & the children to have Daddy away so much, they share it with you of course. But once again you will have your hands very full with hospital and study.

The mailing list cards continue to come in; there will be a higher proportion than I expected, probably because I stamped all the N.Z. ones.

No more just now, much love to you all, from Dad

Kabul
Wednesday evening
3rd September 1970

Dearest Dad

Thank you for your letter of welcome. Well, here we are in Kabul.

Howard drove us in the Bentley to Gatwick airport on a wonderful afternoon, for London. The flight was very good but interrupted

*Monika and the three girls with Blyth, Roger
and Granddad Stan.*

with touchdowns in Frankfurt, Istanbul, Teheran and then Kabul. Faith and Joy slept quite well and Naomi not too badly. I hoped to close my eyes, but it was not possible, maybe too excited. Actually until I saw the different ones at the airport, I had no feeling at all. Rosemary and Ann White were there, John and Betty Strachan, and Noel and Allan Norrish.

We were taken to the spacious house of the Norrish's, very old but homely. We were given two rooms, and are very comfortable. What hit me was the heat, still in the upper 80's F indoors, and the dust; I had forgotten one needed to dust twice a day otherwise you can write on floor and furniture. The children noticed the smell and the flies. Joy was scared stiff of Afghans and their dogs. All we needed was a good sleep.

I went to the service on Sunday evening and received a warm welcome. Many folk are away. On Monday the house hunting started, near the school and church only three houses were in question.

The third was a big old place on the road behind the church. It is near the girls school, the Strachans and closest to the Noor hospital. It looks like a pig-stye at present and needs repairs and painting done. As the position is good I thought I might as well take up the offer. It could become a very nice house, although it would need a lot of furniture to fill it and the fact that it is handy to dump guests in cannot be avoided.

We are all well, but Joy vomited twice last night. She filled her doll's bottle with un-boiled water and drank it. All for today, I have really felt the Lord's help so far.

With much love from us all
Monika

31 Bedford Place
London WC1
20ᵗʰ September 1970

Dearest Dad

How time is flying away! This week will see the end of the FRCS course. It will also have seen Monika's shift into the new house. She wrote that all our household things were scattered and broken. I know that she will be praying for the Lord to give her grace to hold her tongue. She is in fact one of the most discreet women I have met. Years of living as a stranger in foster houses, and later the deaconess house, has given her a sixth sense of what to say and what will hurt people. In the latter respect she is better than I am.

I just heard this afternoon that I can stay on here at the M.M.A. hostel until I return to Kabul. With the end of the most recent car

Our second house in Kabul.

strike it looks as though I might get delivery of the Land Rover before I leave. Two of the boys from the hostel are very keen to come on the trip. I would leave November 1st or 2nd and try to get to Kabul by the 21st. I sent in my entry for the London FRCS exam. Starts on Oct. 19th.

Love, Howard

8 Currie Avenue
Auckland 4
October 20th 1970

Dearest Son

So, life begins at forty! The theme of the learned American professor who wrote a book of that title was, that until forty a man is learning various skills, developing interests, trying his hand at this and that; but at forty he begins the real business of life, has decided what the main stream shall be and should be setting out in real earnest to make the most of the years ahead, shedding all but the essential as he realizes that in one short life one cannot do all that would interest him.

Well for me it began at least twenty years earlier; the poverty of childhood and youth had left its mark, education was scanty, and there seemed to be just two things, working for a living and a concentration on a very narrow circle of Christian interests. Looking back, whilst I'm very thankful for all the goodness of God, I feel how circumscribed life has been and how much I have missed.

So I am thankful that your own path has been cast in wider lines and the years of preparation have been so much longer and richer in experience. Now, as you know, my hope is that the Lord will allow this to be the end of exams with their pressure and that thus freed, the next phase may be service without hindrance where He has called you, and especially that His blessing will be with you in the home.

With November 1st just ahead, the enclosed is that you might get some small thing for your birthday. It will not buy much these days, it was a weeks' wages when I was married!

Thank you for giving me the details of exam dates and subjects, I am following closely in prayer as are a number of the friends here who have asked. You may think me old fashioned, but I hope it may not be on the Sunday and that the day may be one for reflection and dedication.

Now Son, I think I'll run up to the post with this, right now you should be doing the papers on the second day of the exams.

Much love, from Dad

31 Bedford Place
London WC1
November 2nd 1970

Dearest Dad

It was so good to hear your voice on Friday night! Although I knew it was around 4:30am on Saturday morning for you, I felt that you would like to know at once and so phoned straight through on the hostel phone. I sent a cable to Monika but I don't suppose she'll get it for a couple of days.

It was a very low pass rate. I didn't expect to pass after a rather shabby performance in the short cases. In the afternoon they began to call out the results; number 703 was first, then 709 and then my number 710! 703 was a Jordanian whom I knew, so I gave him an Arab bear hug and kissed him on both cheeks. 709 was a NZ boy, none of the other NZ boys passed.

Well I have just written withdrawing my entry for Glasgow. How glad I really am to do that and to know that this whole exam pattern has at last come to an end. How good is the God we adore! I'm still not quite settled in my mind after all this strife and turmoil. I hope the trip back to Kabul will do that for me.

Fondest love
Your Howard

31 Bedford Place
London WC1
8th November 1970

Dearest Dad

It was good to receive two letters from you the other day. The photo certainly takes one back!

What lies ahead in Kabul? This is a cloud to me. In a sense I always felt that the desire of the mission for me to pass the FRCS was not for my benefit or for that of the work, but to put off the awkward moment of my return and the need to take any account of me. The fact that I passed the London FRCS within the specified time will be no cause of rejoicing for them, but rather demolish the mystique enjoyed by J. and H. of possessing recognized qualifications. It will also mean that my opinions will have to be taken account of. This is all sad, for rather than a shotgun marriage I would have wished for a spontaneous relationship of love, fellowship and mutual respect.

It is no use bluffing myself that I am wanted by the mission or for that matter by all the members of NOOR. It will surely be a difficult matter to live with suspicion and misunderstanding, yet the Lord's call is to still "Follow Me". This is one further experience in which I can cry to Him for salvation, wisdom and strength. Also to show real love and forgiveness, something that is not easy, yet Christ-like.

I go tomorrow to the College of Surgeons to sign the book of Fellows, (and pay more money). Then at 11am on Monday set off from Victoria to Dover, Dover to Ostend, and Ostend to Cologne. In Cologne I change trains and go as far as Zagreb where I hope to connect with the boys. They set out on Thursday with the new Land Rover heavily laden with fridge and small freezer, lots of equipment and food.

*The second Land Rover that Howard drove from
England to Afghanistan.*

Yesterday, I sent off a green cardigan for your birthday and a shirt and tie for Christmas. Hope it arrives safely and that no duty is charged. It comes with much love and thankfulness for your continued good health.

This last letter from the U.K. comes with very much love and thanks to you for all your help during the years.

Fondest love, your Howard

Ezerum, Turkey
Tuesday 17th November 1970

My Darling

Well, here we are in Ezerum, just one day from the Iran Border. We came through the centre of Turkey instead of going up to the Black Sea. It saved several days of travel and the road was quite good.

I am writing this by firelight at our camp which is a B.P. petrol station about twenty miles beyond Ezerum. We have just had tea (dried meat, carrots and beans) and are listening to Beethoven's violin concerto. My front is roasting hot and but my back is freezing.

Camping each night has certainly been an experience, but quite cold. Most times we eat one meal a day in the local restaurants and make one meal ourselves. We have a gas cooker and buy things as we go along. Mandarins, oranges and apples are all in good supply at present.

Tomorrow we hope to cross over into Iran and spend the night at Tabriz. I expect we will go to Isfahan for a couple of days to see Ron P. We will then come back up to the Caspian Sea and then through Herat and home.

Much love
Your Howard

Monika.

Chapter 12
Opposition

Howard returning to Afghanistan by Land Rover after passing the FRCS in London.

Kabul

November 21st 1970

Dearest Dad

You may wonder why you have not heard from me for so long. I certainly enjoyed your good letters and followed your moves with great interest.

I am very much hoping that Howard is not too many thousands of miles away. Over a week ago I had a letter from Istanbul. It takes about four days to drive through Turkey via Ankara, four to five days through Iran and two days from the Iranian border to Kabul. He mentioned three co-drivers, all newly qualified doctors. I wonder how long they will stay and whether they have just come for the trip or have a genuine interest in the land.

Today the widow of a certain deceased came to visit. Life has been tough for her; her little girl may have the same condition her husband died of, (bone cancer), and has had one operation and another one due. The mother has come to trust Him, as has one of her brothers, this is wonderful. She is a brave lady, working mornings in the Eye hospital, going to school every afternoon and looking after her girl, mother and a whole lot of other relatives too. I have two spare quilts that I want her to have.

At present I have had my hands full. Faith took sick last week with what seemed to be flu. Six other children, out of eleven in her class are also unwell. However, she had these awful nosebleeds and once they stopped she would be sick from all the blood she had swallowed. I never stopped cleaning up and washing things down. Finally I called Dr. Friesen to check her chest because she complained all the previous night of difficulty in breathing, and sure enough it was pneumonia. Several others from her class also developed the same trouble and other children are sick with hepatitis, of which there is an epidemic this year.

Well I must wash my hair and get some sleep while I can. Are you still visiting old Mrs. Bennett? Please pass on greetings to these old faithful ones. I guess we ought to write a newsletter soon.

Much love from me and the girls
Monika

Herat, Afghanistan
Halleluyah!
Sunday November 24th 1970

Dearest Dad

The day we prayed for has arrived at last! At about midnight last night we rolled into the Afghan border post, with no accidents, no unnecessary delays. Praise God! I felt a pressure lifted off my mind as soon as we rolled away from the border post.

Kabul, Sunday December 6th – My fragmentary comments above were written in Herat a week ago! It doesn't seem that long ago I must say. We arrived in Kabul after dark, about 6:45 pm, to find Monika and the girls all waiting in great excitement. They were all recovering from the flu. I set to and unloaded the Land Rover at once with the help of the boys. The house is really huge with lots of bedrooms, a large study etc, all for £25 a month. It is close to school, church and a couple of miles from the hospital. A good deal of my time was taken up with entertaining the three boys and getting the things I had brought put away.

The day after my arrival it snowed heavily for two days, winter began with a surprising suddenness.

John Strachan was the first to welcome me, closely followed by Ben and Lisa, then Herb and Jock. Christy and Betty came in early next morning, Colin and Gladys came in on Sunday afternoon – all very polite.

The church was well filled, but with fewer AID folk. The new church building still stands unfinished, with only the roof, concrete floor and one end of the building closed in.

I did one morning in the outpatient clinic and it was very busy. The (temporary) hospital is nice. They seem to have got most of the balance of the money now for the building of the NOOR Eye Hospital. Allan is touring Europe for the last $100,000.

Fondest care
Howard

Box 23
Kabul
13th December 1970

Dearest Dad

It is a lovely sunny day, the weather has been cold but clear, crisp and warm during the day. Last night I installed a new Diesel stove that I bought in Mashad (Iran) and I'm glad to say that it is going like a bomb.

As I sit here I wonder again how you would like it here. Ours is a huge house and hard to beat. Right next door the landlord has a three room house that is empty. I was wondering if you would care to move in for some months!

I have plunged into the medical work now. Started operating on Thursday and have been at two busy clinics.

Spiritually there have been two encounters. One was a welcome home dinner given by NOOR hospital, with Afghan and foreign staff present. After prayer and consultation, I decided to read the Beatitudes according to Luke. Basically, I said that I was learning lessons in my life that were much more important than the study for the FRCS. The atmosphere was friendly enough.

The second occasion was the Friday prayer meeting for mission staff. I began by welcoming the progress made in my absence and continued by mentioning the misunderstandings that had arisen in my absence – things had been said by some that were hurtful to me. I said that I frankly forgave them for these. I read Matthew 18 vs 15, "If your brother sins, go and show him his fault in private; if he listens to you, you have won your brother." I reminded them that this scripture had not been followed and that Satan could gain entrance through these affairs; that God knew all my faults, I knew some of them myself, and if any knew more of them and if any felt bitter in their hearts towards me I would be grateful if they would come to me. John Strachan came to me straightaway and told me that I had broken one of the new rules; no one is allowed to speak or address the company without first having permission from the executive secretary.

So far no one has come forward. However, all the same it was a weight off my mind, for it has been impressed on me last year that it was in this area that truth had faltered. Prayer is needed!

Yours, Howard

8 Currie Avenue
Auckland 4
NZ
December 23rd 1970

Dearest Howard and Monika

Well! I was interested to hear of your 'encounters' after arrival. I know it has been in your mind since last year to have a confrontation sometime to try to clear the air, and I am sure it has been a trial of your patience to have to wait so long. You sure put the cat among the canaries! It is one thing to admit one has faults, quite another to ask folk to come and tell you what faults they find. Some would not have the nerve, though they talk to others about you. If they tell you what they see as faults, you will need much grace to receive the criticism graciously. What are faults to them may not seem faults to you, and if you show the slightest resentment, it will make things much worse than if nothing had been said. I wonder if, quite unconsciously, your move was not one to vindicate yourself;

and I still feel it is better to leave one's vindication for the Lord to work out in his own way.

The rule about addresses etc. not being given without the prior consent of the organizing secretary, seems to me a good and fair one, calculated to avoid bickering and back-chat. It applies to ALL who might speak their mind and does not single you out. If you did not know the rule, you can surely explain that, and express your regret at the infraction. I should hope that you did not do it wittingly. You have both been so deeply hurt that it is difficult to avoid being sensitive and perhaps suspicious. Love that thinketh no evil is not possible where the flesh is concerned, only the Holy Spirit can produce it in such circumstances.

As I read the published circulars from Jock and Colin, it seems obvious to me that the mission, in both branches, is now an entirely different set-up from what you and Christy established; you say yourself that the organization is going like a bomb, so they have evidently got out of their muddle and created what amounts to a new set-up, using the old names as they are accepted by the powers that be. It is almost as if in returning, you have joined an interdenominational and international mission.

Mother and I will both be at Blyth's for dinner on Christmas day, I will meet her at the Brown's Bay bus. Oh, Mother has given me $2 for each of the children to be put in their bank accounts, as a Christmas gift.

New Year greeting and much love to you all, from Dad

Mazar-i-Sharif

29th March 1971

Dearest Dad

Well here at last! I suppose this is where I have always wanted to come, this being the last piece of Central Asia such as Mildred Cable and George Hunter knew it. I must say my spirits rose as we left Kabul behind and crossed the mighty 10,000 ft Salang Pass into Central Asia proper.

Mazar is pleasant at this time of year, after Kabul it felt like summer heat here. The hospital is old and falling to bits. However, medically it is more active than most provincial hospitals. The head doctor has tried hard to help us. We have been given two large empty rooms for wards and a small office for outpatients. The rest of the team arrived safely last night. We are now ready to start work and it looks as though we will be busy enough. During this time I hope to cover the cross and resurrection stories at our morning prayers.

The town is full of Russian workers, working on the gas pipeline going into Russia, also on a factory.

Much love from
Howard

Mosque in Mazar-i-Sharif.

8 Currie Avenue
Auckland 4, N.Z.
August 10th 1971

Dearest Howard and Monika

I was glad to get the draft of your circular and realize under what difficulties you wrote it, what with the toothache, work rush, "The Way Out"* and a dozen and one things to do. Well, your circular would be of real interest and many would like to hear its news but the more I have considered it the more I realize it could be explosive! Even if I omitted a number of names, there are many on the mailing list I do not know and in 500 there is bound to be a leak somewhere.

---

* The Way Out was a ministry started to meet the needs of the flood of hippies that passed through Kabul on their way to India in search of peace, freedom and drugs. Many needed medical help.

227

Maybe if this reaches you in time, you could take a quiet hour at Ziarat to make a fresh draft? It takes some of the pep out of it to avoid the use of place names, but also takes away the risk if it got into the wrong hands.

So sorry to add to your burdens, son, but I think it would be better to wait until you have the time rather than send out something less than good.

It is getting late, I was at the Bible reading before writing this, and want it to catch the 11pm mail in hope it may reach you before going on holiday, so will not add more.

Much love to you all from
Dad

Kabul
August 1971

Dear Praying Friends

Looking back over the past months we have much to give praise for, and to report to you who have been carrying the burden with us.

Before furlough much of my time and effort was taken up with planning and building a blind school and eye hospital in Kabul. In my absence the blind school was erected and is being used as a temporary eye hospital of 35 beds. Owing to the good heating the hospital has been very busy all winter and now has a long waiting list. In the past weeks building has began on the main eye hospital, which is next to the blind school.

EYE CAMPS – So far we have been to Kandahar, Mazar-i-Sharif, Faizabad and this week we were at another new place, Yakolang, in the central part of Afghanistan. Of these clinics Mazar, which lies on the border with Russia, was by far the busiest. This work has been largely handicapped by the absence of Rosemary, who had this work on her heart. We are happy to say that she will be back in February.

TRACHOMA CONTROL – 90% of the population are affected by this eye disease at one time or another, untreated it can cause blindness. Our latest project is a public health programme aimed at controlling this disease in school children. Centres are planned for all areas of the country, we trust in each of the four large provincial towns at least and in Kabul, the capital. These are also opportunities for more people called of God to come here.

Rosemary.

BLIND SCHOOL – Monika is starting a series of about thirty health lectures for the blind girls next week, which will need a lot of preparation as they will be given in Persian. Opportunities for witness will naturally occur during the lectures.

Monika with two blind students.

NOOR NEWS – You may remember that our eye work took the name of NOOR, which in Persian means "light" in the spiritual sense. We are now twenty two workers strong from eight countries. Allan is the executive secretary and Herb (an ophthalmologist from the USA) is the project director. This has left my hand freer for the work we most wish to do, the nurturing of the infant ekklesia.* Here there have been definite moves forward in the past months. Four people have followed the example of the Ethiopian Treasurer. However, almost at once a severe temptation befell some in regard to honesty. There is a suggestion to secure a long leasehold property which could be used for a fellowship center and also a residence. Pray for guidance in this regard.

HIPPIE HOTEL – Friends from the local foreign church have rented the top two floors of a downtown hotel. It was an ideal place for contacting the thousands of hippies pouring through Kabul in search of hashish and other drugs. What a thrill it was to see many come up to the hotel every night for discussion. More than twelve made a stand at this time, some were delivered from drugs such as heroin.

PERSONAL NEWS – We have all been on holiday to Ziarat.

---

* ekklesia – Greek for church

This is a small hill station in Baluchistan, close to Quetta. There is a mission bungalow that we were able to rent cheaply. We greatly benefited from the peace and quiet. It has been a hot and dusty summer with no rain at all since March, the country is parched and a drought has been declared. Please pray for rain.

Next week Naomi starts fourth grade, Faith second and Joy goes for the first time to school; we will sadly miss this little one from the house, we have much enjoyed her company.

With love in the Lord from us all,
Yours Howard and Monika

Baptism of new believers, former Hippies.

PO Box 23, Kabul
Afghanistan
12 February 1972

Dearest Dad

The days have ticked by without any chance to sit down and write a letter. It has been a difficult time for us.

First of all to give some of the events of the past couple of weeks. Since last writing I have been down to Farah with John, we were asked to distribute about £1500 worth of aid to victims of a fairly serious flood. The KCCC, (Kabul Community Christian Church), had this sum of money given to them by a former member for use in this way.

John Strachan buying relief supplies.

On the Thursday we went around the bazaar in Kandahar, hired a truck and bought a couple of thousand old overcoats. Each over-coat cost about £1 and some were very good quality indeed, though long and old fashioned. We also purchased 1000 tins of cooking fat. We then got clearance from the customs authorities before taking off in the late afternoon for Farah. The flood had thrown down many of the houses, which were just pools of mud; about 1600 had been destroyed. We met the Governor, who knew me quite well, as his sister is the wife of our former landlord. He was most helpful and undertook to give out the coats together with the help coming in from the Red Cross etc. They had a real system going for distribution, with lists of people in need and a slow but systematic distribution to them.

Distribution of overcoats to refugees from flood disaster.

While I was away things had blown up, both Allan and Herb on the war path. The events leading up to this most recently was that I had been asked by the Ministry of Health to assist them in preparation of a five year plan of developing ophthalmology in Afghanistan. Working to a deadline I had only got the draft of the plan finished the day before it was due and then gave it over to Allan and Herb before presenting it to the Ministry of Health. There was a violent reaction and instead of presenting this plan, we presented another which only covered the year ahead and the work in Herat. Herb said that he felt I could never accept his leadership, and Allan also opened fire with some well founded criticisms. The result of it was that I agreed to accept their demands and try for a better relationship. Out of all of this I hope I learn something, but I don't know, every year it is getting harder for the leopard to change his spots! There is no doubt it has taken me a long time to get over the '69 events. Like Mum I am a slow forgiver, perhaps never. I also always tend to get far too involved in things and do not finish things properly. Well, the Lord knows these things and much besides! My trust is that He will transform these hindrances.

The other thing is that I decided not to go ahead with the land purchase for the fellowship centre.

So much to say, so little space! I wish I could have spent more time writing to you, but I found these troubled weeks, the last two with not much joy in them. Monika, I know, has also found it difficult.

It has been very cold, with much snow falling even in Kabul, several feet have fallen over the past three weeks, the most they've had in years. It was also cold in Kandahar.

Yours
Howard

8 Currie Avenue
Auckland, 4 N.Z.
February 24th 1972

My dearest Son,

Your letter of the 12th was very welcome to-day, I had began to think that there may be something brewing, or that perhaps one of you may be unwell, and am not surprised to hear of the active time you have had. Though the heavy snowfall may be the cause of distress at the time, it may turn out for good in the long run, in supplying needed moisture for the short summer season of growth, especially in the higher altitudes in the centre of the country. Miss Bate mentioned the shortage of both snow and rain during the past two years, and the hardships and hunger of the poor.

Yes, I recall your earlier visit to Farah, when you mentioned poverty, dust and flies; poor souls, they would be thankful for any relief; the length of the overcoats would be an advantage rather than a drawback.

I'm so sorry you have had such a trying time and the prospect of a flare-up with Allan and Herb. Over the years I have told you your faults so often and plainly that it is a wonder you have not dropped me entirely; yet you have taken it and loved me just the same. It has taken me a long time to realize that I can do nothing to help you overcome the characteristics you have, which so provoke others that they miss seeing your many good qualities and lose patience.

I must say that I think things would run more smoothly if you had NOTHING to do with planning and organizing for NOOR and confined yourself to ophthalmology and dealing with needy souls, thus accepting the direction of Herb and Allan as to medical activities. I suppose that is what would be involved if you had a position at Moorfields or Auckland!

You said regarding conditions there, and the difficulty regarding complete forgiveness of others, "My trust is that He will transform these hindrances". Somehow, son, I don't think He does anything for us that He has told us to do ourselves. If He commands us to do something, we must DO it, not pray about it.

It is likely, I think, that the decision to drop the property project will prove a good one; there have been too many "ifs and buts" about it, and that is not usually characteristic of a scheme that the LORD is engineering.

How comforting it is that however much we may be misunderstood, He knows, loves, cares and is working all together for our good and His glory! The Lord make this a very fruitful chapter of your life!

Much love from
Dad

8 Currie Avenue
Auckland, 4 N.Z.
February 27th 1972

Dearest Son

I had scarcely posted No.9 when I wished I hadn't! So far as I recall it hadn't a single word of encouragement for you in the trying time you are passing through, and reflected instead my own depression that you have been going through the mill again. If I had held it for twenty four hours I don't think it would have gone. I can only hope that it did not add to your difficulties and that it did not sound fault-finding from this end – I didn't mean it to be so.

I look back with constant thanksgiving for the grace of God in you, and your response to it; if you have not been specially gifted with what is necessary for the functional organizing machinery of a mission, He has given you richly some of the personal qualities that enable you to approach others with a warm and generous heart that secures their response. You have been patient with trying folk and have not turned back from the work to which you were called. The words of David Barber in the Westminster Echo so long ago, revealed that you had the Master's gentle touch in dealing with the needy. As for me, life would have been unspeakably lonely without your continual thoughtfulness for me. So often when you wrote you must have been so desperately weary that I felt guilty in the pleasure of receiving letters!

That is poor comfort to offer when there is the unspeakable love of Christ ever active toward you, His assurance that the Father Himself loveth you, and He is working all together for good, even the things we look on as mistakes.

"Faint not, nor fear, His arm is near;
  He changeth not, and thou art dear,
  Only believe and thou shalt see
  That Christ is all in all to thee."

Now I think that is all just now; you know that you are all constantly in my thoughts and prayers.

Much love to you all from
Dad

PO Box 23
Kabul, Afghanistan
March 5th 1972

Dearest Dad

Many thanks for your letter giving advice about recent events here in Kabul. I must say, "Great minds think alike". Much of what you said has already been said by Monika, particularly the advice to abstain from administrative activities, which seems to have riled Allan and Herb (possibly rightly!).

Things seem to be running more smoothly at the moment, this may well be because we are not doing much work, it has been quite slack at the hospital during these days thus giving us plenty of time to do other things. After this sort of fracas I received a new title, NOOR planning officer. I am not too sure what this means, but have been putting some work into planning the Herat Hospital. This has been going ahead quite fast.

Today is the last day of the interim-pastor for the KCCC, (Kabul Christian Community Church). It has been a good, practical sort of ministry with some fruit over the past six months.

Later today – I just returned from the KCCC where they had five baptisms and two dedications of infants. They used the new baptistery which was still unfinished and the new building was very cold indeed. The fancy heating blew all the fuses in the nearby transformer; it is the under-floor heating type.

Interestingly enough, others have been making suggestions to me, one is that as I am a doctor I should stick to doctoring and have nothing to do with spiritual work; this is used to keep the idea of the fellowship centre down! However, my answer to that is frankly this is not me! I never set out to be that sort of doctor and if doctoring gets in the way of the other work, it would eventually have to go.

I don't see this at the present time, as it still seems to be the key to open many doors here.

Tuesday- I just received your good letter following up your previous one. No, I don't think you did wrong by sitting down and writing what came to you. It is no use hiding your disappointment from me, I knew well enough that what I had to write would not be good news for you or for anyone else for that matter. Certainly I have had little enough of encouraging words from anyone during these last three years. One thing after another! Yet somehow I have a feeling that trying to act sincerely, and according to my own inward light, will in the end prove to be the most honest and profitable way. I never could stand hypocrisy.

Love from us all, yours, Howard

Chapter 13
Expulsion

Narrow gorge in Northern Afghanistan.

Kabul, Afghanistan
October 1972

Dear Praying Friends

As I look out of my office window I see the shadows are lengthening and the days getting shorter. Already at night the frost has killed off our abundant display of anemones, and the morning glory which covers the front of our porch is producing less and less flowers every morning. It is a reminder to me of you all, that not since the beginning of the year have I set pen to paper to report clearly to you of the Lord's doings in and through us. You will understand that our situation is such that we simply cannot afford publicity if we are to remain effective workers in this land, yet our need for intelligent prayer is supreme, as there is just so much going on and so many perplexing situations we face.

HIGHLIGHT – of the year was to participate in the burial and resurrection services of three local believers, and ten world travelers, many of the latter were hippies who had been delivered from hard drugs such as heroine. Praise God for His wonderful works in this far away and forgotten place! He is seeking to make up for the hundreds of years in which the name of Christ has not been known here.

FELLOWSHIP CENTRE – There was a period when it seemed this idea might die due to lack of finance, and permission to get a lease for the land. However about month ago it looked as if we would have the 99 year lease signed, an agreement was reached quickly with the Land Bank and the owner; all seemed clear. Suddenly, however, the Foreign Ministry came into the picture and demanded that the Ministry of Justice be consulted and the matter passed onto the cabinet. We are waiting to see how the Lord will answer this fresh complication. Thank you for all your generous and sacrificial gifts towards this centre.

*The KCCC church
(A-framed building in background).*

HIPPIES – I helped this summer with the clinic for hippies and other world travelers, run under the name of Dilaram House by Floyd and Sally, a fine young couple from Texas.

REFUGEES – I was asked to serve on a relief committee set up by the KCCC in order to assist in a very serious famine situation in the middle of the country, Hazarajat. This high part of Asia, mostly over 8000ft, has long cold winters with temperatures going down to 50°F. To make matters worse, for three years they have had little rain and thus very small wheat crops. Their animals died or were eaten during the last cruelly cold winter. Hundreds of people have lost their lives in the famine and thousands lost all their livelihood and homes. The church felt we must help. First of all we had an eye clinic there, which we combined with a feeding programme for starving children and women. Some of the children looked like living skeletons at the start of our work. Over the summer Rosemary and Robert were able to minister effectively to about three hundred of these poor people, as well as set up a home for 16 orphaned boys and 10 widowed women, most of these were living in caves close to the administrative centre of the province. The government launched quite a large operation to get wheat into the area before the passes close in a month.

KCCC – this is the only such group officially permitted in this land. A couple of years back they began to erect a beautiful church to the design of Tom H. of Auckland. It is almost completed now. About a month ago I got a phone call to come at once, as the church was being attacked. Sure enough, outside there was a squad of workmen from the municipality demolition team with orders to destroy the church. The Lord gave help however, and a phone call to the Mayor of Kabul, who is an eye patient of ours, brought a short halt in the demolition. The American Ambassador then was able to speak to the King, who ordered no further action. The matter still is not settled and needs prayer and patience. There is no other church in Afghanistan.

MINISTRY OF THE WORD – this has gone on quietly twice a week with our small group and individually with interested ones. It was a great joy for me to welcome back Christy Wilson after a year in the States, he is an able minister of God's word and a true friend in Christ. He is still trying to get his residence visa.

WARNINGS – Several times during the past months friends in high places in the government warned me directly and indirectly

New Blind School in Kabul, first used as an Eye Clinic.

that we are in danger of being expelled from the country and even of physical harm. So far the Lord has His hand over us and we are not afraid. It is a sign that the Lord is able even to take our tiny light and use it here for His glory. We will stay here as long as He wants us here!

BUILDING – the new 90 bed eye hospital has nearly been completed by the German contractors. It is a beautiful unit. NOOR hopes to move over early in the New Year.

HOME – We had the pleasure of a family holiday during the summer. We went camping up a beautiful river in Pakistan and I went fishing each day. The girls are now back at school, Monika keeps busy with the home and her work in the Blind School. Thankfully we are all well.

Yours in our Lord Jesus,
Howard and Monika

Naomi, Faith and Joy riding in the Kaghan Valley, Pakistan.

Karachi, Pakistan
December 26th 1972

Dearest Dad

We have been thinking a lot of you during these days and wondering what you are doing with yourself over Christmas.

We have just completed our time at the beach and can say that it has been a real benefit. Personally, when I came down to Karachi I felt washed out. The continued strain with the mission and not knowing whether we were out or in had a curious effect on me which I don't remember before, namely that I began to be somewhat forgetful. Also on the trip down from Peshawar on the train (it takes two nights and a day) I developed dysentery.

On arrival in Karachi we went out to the Pittmans, (Baptists), who control the renting of the beach hut, and then straight out to the beach. I did not even think to get an air-letter form to write to you. Thus for seven days we were almost alone on the beach, just ourselves, my books, the sea, long walks along the sandy beach and the radio. I felt my mind click back into action about the third day and now feel completely back to normal once more.

Beach hut in Karachi.

246

*The girls enjoy the company of a monkey
at Sandspit beach.*

My daily programme was to get up each day about 7am and
walk for two hours, about six miles all together I guess. During this
time I read the Psalms. After breakfast I played night-man, as there
are no toilet facilities and we used a bucket. A local lad brought
water in 4 gallon cans for us as needed. After this I settled down
to read my philosophy textbook, which I read more than halfway
through, from Aristotle to Descartes – pretty dry stuff. I also read a
couple of interesting books on Afghanistan and Central Asia.

I also, of course, prayerfully considered the question of the mission, but came to no different conclusion, namely we should resign.
I will be seeing Robbie Orr tomorrow and staying overnight with
them so will hear what he has to say. He was, of course, at the mission
meetings and may have some further light to throw on proceedings,
and advice to give; this I will listen to respectfully as always.

The only fresh thought I had at the seaside was that it might be time to begin systematic instruction of the promising believers; a course which would eventually cover a bible school syllabus. The releasing of the mission ties would provide time to do this. We had about thirty along to our house the night before we left for Karachi; it was encouraging to see the maturity and growth of some.

Love from us all
Yours, Howard

8 Currie Avenue
Auckland 4, N.Z.
February 21ˢᵗ 1973

Dearest Son

Tonight I'm tired, as usual in the warm evenings, but I think that I had better try to record a few lines before I forget what was in the letter Stewart Hillman showed me this afternoon. He did not show me Allan's letter to Wiremu Street brethren, only the copy Allan had sent of his letter to the blind mission that support you. In this he referred at length to the continued difficulty they have with Dr Harper, and said they wished the blind mission to know that they would be discussing your future relationship with the mission at the May meetings. Allan also referred to their lengthy discussions at the last executive meeting held in Kabul. I will try to condense their grounds for complaint – it was a two page letter and my memory for detail is not what it was.

First then, is the fact that you do not seem to be able to accept the directives of the executive and the rule of the appointed leaders. Second, he says that you tend to attempt too much, dividing your time and energies between various programmes; he mentions the relief and church programmes, and that in developing these you threw an undue burden on other workers in NOOR because you gave less time there and more to the new programmes. He spoke of their insistence that you drop the chairmanship of the church committee. He acknowledged your many good qualities and vision in seeing things that needed to be done, but really the crux of his whole complaint is your independence of executive detail.

Wiremu Street is very much reduced in numbers and they are in the process of trying to pull things together. They held a church meeting recently and the set up of elders is Stewart Hillman, Fred and Gordon, and three deacons (they were only children when you left NZ). They have gone over the matter, decided to continue to stand behind you and are of the opinion that it is probably the time when you might consider working independently of the mission, if that is possible, as it seems unlikely that you will be able to harmonize with the executive.

I am so grateful to the Lord that He is enabling you to accept all without bitterness of spirit and resentment; nothing can harm you if He has first place. One can't help feeling hurt, but as you commit your reactions to Him, He will keep you in perfect peace down at the centre, even when contrary winds are blowing up at the surface.

In 1969 the mission tried to get rid of you with false charges of misconduct and failed; now they are trying to wear you down on disobedience to written regulations. It seems to me that you have tried your utmost to accept their directives, and whatever 'offence' you have committed in their sight has been unintentional on your part.

Much love, from Dad

Kabul

March 26th 1973

Dearest Dad

Brother Christy W. has just departed for the USA, so I will concentrate on giving you a worm's eye view of the events of the last weeks. Perhaps it would be better to give a chronicle, as it will avoid verbosity.

Feb 24th – I went by plane to Iran, to work with Professor Barrie Jones in trachoma control. The American ambassador travelled on the same plane.

Feb 25th – Back in Kabul, at 2 pm about two hundred workmen plus equipment came to the Kabul Community Church (KCCC) and knocked down the rest of the wall. Christy Wilson managed to get a one week stay of demolition from the Supreme Court in Kabul.

March 5th – I began to travel back from Bandar Abbas to Mashad, Iran. Meanwhile in Afghanistan the KCCC board met and made a suggestion to Christy Wilson that he should leave the country, based largely on advice from the American ambassador.

March 6th – Arrived in Mashad, Iran.

March 7th – Crossed the border between Iran and Afghanistan and travelled to Herat. I discovered that my presence was urgently required in Kabul. The blind school had been closed on order of the Acting Minister of Health. Blind school workers were served with one week expulsion orders which were later extended to ten days.

March 9th – Closure and disbandment of blind schools in Herat and Kabul, and dismantling of all equipment. At the afternoon KCCC board meeting Christy Wilson announced his decision to leave the country, with the hope of coming back as soon as the storm had settled.

Outside the Blind School in Kabul.

March 22nd – Received your letter, telling of the strong reaction from Wiremu Street elders in our support.

March 24th – A dark day for Afghanistan, Christy Wilson and Betty left in the morning. It marked the end of an era and one felt the unifying factor in both the mission and KCCC had left. The manner of his going, not at the direct wish of the Afghans, saddened me. I went home and took to my bed with a slight dose of the flu.

March 30th – Allan and Gordon just came over, they had an answer from the Administrative Council to my letter, regarding my resignation, that had suggested three courses of action. They simply want me to resign. This alternative means that I have no further links with the Mission and am free to make my own arrangements with the Afghan government for future work in this country. Of the three alternatives I gave them, I think they have chosen the worst. It is almost inevitable that it will lead to division, recriminations and is a bad testimony to the Afghans. I have striven to avoid this and would have preferred an agreed separation, with the Mission voluntarily

251

relinquishing the trachoma control project, and myself and the Mission living in some kind of symbiosis. However, instead of this Allan has left me free before the Lord to negotiate something new. Well, this is not my wish, and I can only commit myself into God's hands now and quietly go forward and see what He will do. I will strive to live in harmony with the brothers from the Mission as long as they are left in the country and if I am meant to continue here.

Yesterday morning I woke with a vile headache and a premonition of evil; this morning there is peace. The mission tunnel has been a long, tortuous and dark one. I trust the Lord has something simpler ahead of us. May He give us the grace to avoid further entanglements and to crucify any restless ambitions or work in my own strength, but to quietly accept what He has for us.

There is no doubt that the Prime Minister has been eyeing us and would have liked to get us out of the country; it could mean we will have to leave. However God is sovereign and He will direct.

I have written the above letter in this form so that as the events occurred I could get a record of them. I would say that almost all of the information is highly confidential but you could show the letter to close friends for prayer at this time.

Loving greetings
Howard

8 Currie Avenue
Auckland 4, N.Z.
May 4th 1973

Dearest Son

The April diary arrived a few days ago per Mrs. Wilson at Duarte in California, but as I have explained to Monika, I have been stupid with a cold and cannot comment at length on its matter. It gives a running account of doings and, as you know, will be filed with your other letters, so would be available if ever you wish to refresh your memory on any points.

It would be good if one could stand off and see the situation and events as a whole, and know what principles of missionary work have been involved and what lessons there are to be learned. At present you are too much in the midst of things to see them in perspective and I am too weary to trust my judgment to set some conclusions in order for consideration. Sorry, but that is how it is!

I have no doubt that the Lord will over- rule the mistakes that have been made and that He is preparing a way for you, and for all of you, that will glorify Him.

I hope that whatever happens you will not set up another organization, only to suffer a similar experience. You are not, and I repeat, you are not organizationally minded and never will be. You cannot understand that, and may not believe it.

The CMML pattern allows for an independent personality or rugged individualist to do an individual work. Those who come to help are also independent and not tied to an organization. This limits the extent of the work expanding, but it is a limitation due to the personality of the worker and to the acceptance of non-organization and one has to accept that limitation.

I do hope the children are able to finish their year's work at

Ahlman Academy and I am much exercised for them and Monika, as no doubt you are. The Lord REIGNETH! Hallelujah!

Much love from
Dad

P.O. Box 650
Kabul
Afghanistan
May 22nd 1973

Dearest Dad

I hardly know how to write about the many events which have taken place during the past weeks because they have left me just about speechless. One thing I do know is that the Lord is good and He is a rock that cannot be moved, and one does well to put your feet upon that sure ground when the storms of life are raging. The tremendous measure of peace of heart which He poured out upon my soul before the ordeal started, has and is seeing me through.

At times I've felt like just coming home to live a normal life and never to come out here again. If we look at the circumstances, like Peter, we begin to sink, but with faith and eyes on the Savior we can walk on the water. One week looked so black; I received a sad note from foster mother, she is failing fast now, and another letter from Barbara saying she was in hospital again, our resignation from the Mission was handed in and accepted and came into effect immediately, (the realization that things are all over and Howard without work came as a great shock), the sad good-bye to the dear three trachoma control workers (with whom we were close but all three felt it right to continue in the Mission), and those two evenings with the blind mission folk resulted in complete cut of our support. The only time my anger got the better of me was when they suggested we needed four to six months of psychological treatment in India and then to move and work in another country. It seems to be a modern conclusion for everyone who does not fit into the common mould.

I am so glad that our family life has been preserved all this time and the girls seem happy and secure. Also not much has spoiled the very good relationship with the Afghan people. It was dreadful to say goodbye in the hospital, many started to weep. Yet something is not as it ought to be if one has such difficulty in getting along with fellow European workers.

We both felt it was right to resign and stay here until the Lord shows us the way out.

I feel so sleepy these days, but we are all well. Hope you are getting over your cold.

Very much love
Monika

No Fixed Abode!
June 5th 1973

Dearest Dad

Well it looks as if we have joined the nomads! Yesterday I was ordered to present myself at the Kabul Police Headquarters and was given an exit visa to leave the country by Wednesday 6th. The official reason given was that I had "finished my work". The Ministry of Health knew nothing about the expulsion order and they were surprised when I told them. They were still working on a new contract for me and were going to present it to the Prime Minister this Wednesday. Dr. Rex was ordered to leave at the same time.

At the moment I am trying to get an extension on this time to enable us to settle our affairs properly. Then we are not sure whether we will head for Teheran or Pakistan. I expect Teheran, by road. However, I believe that the door will reopen here later. The Lord knows better.

Will keep in touch
Love in Him
Howard

Chapter 14
Relocation

Outside the Missionary Home, Romford, England.

8 Currie Avenue
Auckland 4, N.Z.
June 17th 1973

My dearest Howard and Monika

Yours of June 5th announcing 'no fixed abode' did not take me by surprise, as the evening before Enid told me by toll call that she had word from Christy Wilson to say that you and Rex had notice of instant removal and the church building was to be demolished commencing June 13th.

You and Monika had the honor of being used of the Lord for the opening of the door and the establishment of that which has enabled others to enter. You have had the joy of seeing a number trust the Lord, and have helped in the KCCC. It seems likely to me that the medical work will continue, but under conditions imposed by the government and without looking for folk to be brought to the Lord. As such it would continue to draw financial support, as humanitarian work always does. The future of the nationals who believed is in His hand; some will suffer and all will need our prayers.

You will guess how my imagination worked overtime when I first heard the news, and how concerned I felt for all of you. The realization of what it meant to you to be thrust out, the grief that you were being wrenched away from those you have fellowshipped with and led to Him and have been helping; the break with those you have fellowshipped with at the church; the breaking up of the home, and the interruption for the girls in their schooling and what it will mean for them to leave friends they have made. Then the task of disposing of household goods, of sorting and packing what you can get onto the Land Rover with five passengers and the going out to make a new beginning. Like Abraham, who went out not knowing whither he went!

Yet God is faithful, and though I am still deeply concerned and feel the uncertainty which attends not knowing where you are or where you are going, He has fulfilled the word He gave me from Isaiah 26 "Thou wilt keep him in perfect peace whose mind is stayed on Thee, because he trusteth in Thee."

So many thoughts crop up in prayer, the need of guidance, of financial provision, of accommodation, of safety in travel, food by the way, but He knows all about it and as the Good Shepherd goes before when He puts forth His own sheep.

Much love to you all, Dad.

*Rebel Tanks Guard Kabul**
19.7.73

NZPA – Reuter New Delhi

… Tanks are guarding the main buildings in Kabul, the Afghanistan capital, after a coup which ousted King Mohammed Zahir Shah.

General Sadar Mohamed Daud, a brother-in-law of the King, led the coup and immediately clamped martial law on the country and declared the mountain kingdom a republic.

Afghanistan appears to be sealed off from the outside world, with telephone lines cut and airfields closely guarded.

Shots Heard
Kabul Radio, which broke the news of the coup, did not mention

---

* A newspaper article found amongst the letters describing the coup that took place in Afghanistan just over a month after the expulsion of Howard and the family.

259

bloodshed but diplomatic sources said that small arms fire, explosions and Air Force jets could be heard around the capital.

An American Embassy report said there had been gun-fighting in Kabul Central Prison, which is also the police headquarters and busloads of police were seen being taken away under military escort.

General Daud told the country yesterday that he and his supporters had ousted the King when they saw that their hopes for political reform had gone and that the regime had become corrupt "to such an extent that there was no longer any hope of reforming it."

Meanwhile, King Zahir Shah, has arrived in Rome from an island off Naples. The King went straight to the Afghan Embassy. Spokesmen would not give any details."

Teheran, Iran
July 23rd 1973

Dearest Dad

Well, our time and money are running out here! I thought I had enough money with me to last several months but did not reckon on several very expensive car repairs. Apart from that we have spent money only on food and petrol, having actually quite a cheap place to stay.

The coup in Afghanistan came as a great surprise to us. We did not ever expect that Daud would take over, though I always felt that it would be the army officers that would overthrow the King. I just don't know how they will ever be able to cope with the complex problems of taking a nation forward. Politically, of course, any stability Afghanistan had was with the King, who seems to have accepted what has happened. Well, it leaves us once more with a question mark. We feel now that the way has cleared to this extent; that we should go back to Kabul and see if we are wanted by the new regime. It could be that they will be looking for any help they can get now, to impress people that they are doing something. We have been following each event as it has developed with anxious interest. Apparently the airline has started work again. I heard today that the borders have reopened.

As time is running out for the girls' schooling to be decided, I think we should, in faith, go back to Kabul soon. It should be obvious fairly quickly which way things will go for us. If there is no opening in Afghanistan then we will return to Iran for a short time, after arranging the disposal of anything left in Kabul – piano, fridges, books and clothes.

Much love from us all
Yours Howard

P.O. Box 650
Kabul, Afghanistan
August 23rd 1973

Dearest Dad

Here we are once again! It was a historic moment when we crossed the border of the Republic of Afghanistan after the trip from Teheran.

We packed the car once more and got away to a leisurely start through the thick Teheran traffic. We climbed slowly into the Alborz mountains and were thankful that the traffic was no heavier than it was. After a rather restless night at a dirty motor camp we pressed on the next day to Mashad. Again we stayed with Miss Harvey. For the first time we both felt challenge and opportunity. I went to the Medical School and found that the department of Ophthalmology is very weak. The professor is an older man concerned with his private practice, the actual beds are filled with cataracts only and there is no teaching going on of any sort. He was very pleased to see me and wanted me to help as Assistant Professor. As far as the things that matter most, there is a wide open door there and we could see fruitful service in Iran, if not here in Afghanistan.

We came across the border into Afghanistan with no special trouble. It was good to see Robert and Rosemary again in good spirits. They had all our things which had not been sold and have put us up in their little flat, which only has four rooms.

I at once went to see our old Afghan friends and have been working away on our possible stay. At the moment we await the decision of the Foreign Ministry as to whether we get a visa or not to reside here. The girls in any case start school on Monday which is the opening of the new school year. Once the question of our stay is clear we will begin to look for somewhere to stay; it would be wonderful to settle down once more. Personally we are well and at peace although not sure how things will turn out.

Love from us all, In Him,
Howard

Iranian border post on Afghan border.

P.O. Box 650,
Kabul
September 9th 1973

Dearest Dad

Three weeks have passed since we came back into the country and we have one more week on our tourist visa!

The Lord is keeping us waiting until almost the last minute before anything is revealed to us. This has not been an easy time for us. We have been squashed up in this tiny flat with Robert and Rosemary, and all of our old luggage. We have slowly sorted it through but because it is so cramped we have not been able to make spectacular progress. All I know is that we have about 16 trunks and this is a tenth of what we had in June. Thus like Job, on whom I spoke to a group the other day, we are experiencing a time of shrinking. We do not even have what we had when we left the UK in 1966, namely enough pots and pans etc. to set up house. Well, praise Him for this, for it does not worry either of us.

I have found it most trying just to sit around and wait, and in this too He is working to show me patience. Day after day slips by with little accomplished. I have now written to several places regarding a job, if nothing turns up here. I still would like to come and see you, whatever happens in the near future. However until something becomes clear to us I do not wish to move from here. If necessary I will cable to you when money is needed for the ticket. We are still very interested in Mashad, Iran.

Love from us all
Yours
Howard

P.O. Box 650,
Kabul, Afghanistan
September 30th 1973

Dearest Dad

Another week has passed and still I am not sure that we have seen the light at the end of the tunnel, yet there has been some progress made in some ways.

I made a trip to Jalalabad on Tuesday and had a warm welcome from the eye doctor (who was in the first class that I took there in 1966) and also the Dean of the Medical School there. They did give me an invitation to lecture and work there. The other possibility is of doing corneal grafting work. I would have to raise the eyes from abroad. I think that this together with the long neglected language study would keep me busy. It would mean that I would possibly get my visa through the university.

Despite this uncertainty we have gone ahead with unpacking to a limited extent. After only having camping equipment for a week we took Christy's furniture to look after it for him until his return, so now the house is full of furniture. We are all happy with the new house. It is a little on the small side, but otherwise good. It is centrally situated and sunny yet with lots of trees, some of them fruit trees.

Weather is cooling fairly rapidly now although it has not dropped below freezing yet. The month of fasting is on and this means that work is much curtailed in these days.

Much love from us all
Yours
Howard

Last house in Kabul, in Karte Char area.

P.O. Box 650
Kabul, Afghanistan
October 14th 1973

Dearest Dad

Well, never a dull moment here! Yesterday the government took over the administration of NOOR hospital. Without warning they installed their own administrator and informed the hospital staff they were taking over the hospital "lock, stock and barrel"! It remains to be seen what this exactly means, but whatever, it is a new era for the hospital.

As far as we are concerned I can only feel some joy that we have been completely taken out of things at this time, the Lord surely knows what anguish it might have been to me, and thus chose another way to get us out of things. As it was, the news came to

266

me without the slightest feeling on my part, only a curious thankfulness and praise for the ways of God, which are always hard to understand and yet refreshing. It has also somehow brought to an end the long controversy with the Mission for there is now nothing to have a controversy over!

Our own news seems small fry, but after all that long effort all that has come out for us has been a two month extension to our tourist visa. This will carry us through to the middle of December. It is embarrassing, for really speaking I am not supposed to work on a tourist visa and on the basis of the promise of a visa I had started work. I will be taking this up with the authorities during the week.

Another curious thing is that no post at all has come through from NZ for about two weeks. This could be just a coincidence, but the mail from the UK has been very scanty during the same time. Monika still has not unpacked the cases we had decided to take home!! She really wonders if our time abroad is not over for the time being. However I have not given up.

My math has never been very good and it appears that I had you at 80 years before you had arrived! Perhaps next year we can be there for the great celebration. This year it looks unlikely.

Fondest love from us all
In Him, yours, Howard

P.O. Box 650
Kabul, Afghanistan
November 11th 1973

Dearest Dad

Like you we have certainly had many moments of uncertainty the last few months. It has almost been like the big dipper, at one moment we seem to be riding high, then the next swoosh, we are down at the bottom again and back to square one! I have been advised by friends who "know", that I should just sit quiet for about six months, content to accept the status quo with no clarity regarding my position at Jalalabad, nor with a proper residence visa.

I have been pondering over the fact that there are plenty (or let's say several) people in the world like myself that share a burden for Central Asia. With a fairly long experience now of different situations, my vision once more is extending to the places that I first clearly saw were for me; namely Mongolia, Turkestan and Tibet. I have a strong feeling that I should be using the talent given to me in seeing and seizing opportunities for others to enter in these different areas and then in conjunction with others seeking to provide a loose framework of fellowship (Central Asian Fellowship) for the encouragement and support of such lonely ones. This would be to take up where the Cables and Miss French, George Hunter and Percy Mather, and Mr. Sturt had to leave off. Well, please remember this. As usual my head is full of ideas, most of which are not practical.

We have started fires now, one diesel stove all day, with a wood fire at night. The autumn colours are lovely.

Much love from us all
Yours
Howard

Bus going up to Salang Pass.

January 9th 1974

CENTRAL ASIAN FELLOWSHIP – (Dad, for private circulation not to be published)

In any generation there is a small group of people called to undertake the seemingly impossible for God. One such task is the evangelization of the vast area of Central Asia, which stretches from the cold steppes of Siberia to Mongolia, Tibet, Chinese and Russian Turkestan and down to Afghanistan.

It is an area where the Church of Jesus Christ is at its weakest numerically and where there are severe restrictions on the open proclamation of the gospel. No organized mission group will be permitted in the foreseeable future to undertake work in these areas and yet these huge nations of people, the Mongolians, the Uzbeks, the Turkomen, the Tadjiks, the Khirgiz, the Tibetans, the Pathans are dying without a chance to hear anything but lies about the God who loved them so much He gave His Son for their salvation.

The people called to this task of evangelism face peculiar difficulties. Often they are alone, without fellowship, sometimes imprisoned, sick and discouraged. In many cases they are without the basic Scriptures in the different languages.

There is an upsurge of love and interest in real service for Jesus by the younger generation. Surely God will challenge some of this group to attempt the impossible and pay the price of working for Him in Central Asia. How can we help them in this task? It would be inappropriate to establish yet another mission and try and impose on this huge area the administration and utter inflexibility of such a system, with its bureaucracy, costly overheads, slow moving bumbling committees and continuous need for publicity to keep the machine financed. However, workers in Central Asia do have a need for fellowship of a spiritual nature, a venue to meet and discuss ideas and problems of their work, opportunity for united prayer, workshops to produce suitable literature and to discuss Scripture translation and distribution, detailed information about how to enter different countries, pitfalls to avoid, the provision of a courier service for literature and equipment, medical care etc.

How can we help? I feel at the moment there is a slight relaxation concerning the entry of foreigners into Central Asia. Tourists can now go to every large city in the area, with the exception of Lhasa. Students can go to many of these areas to study language.

In order to assist with these needs it is proposed that a Central Asian Fellowship be established. Membership would be open to all evangelical Christians called by God to work in this area. Submitted on behalf of my beloved Central Asia, Howard.

8 Currie Avenue
Auckland 4, N.Z.
January 19ᵗʰ 1974

Dearest Howard and Monika

Early in the week I received the outline of Central Asian Fellowship, which I read with interest and it will be shown to those whom I think may be interested. I am very conscious these days that the world I belonged to has vanished and that I am unable to adjust my thinking to many present day activities. That being so, I hesitate to evaluate new movements except as regards scriptural principles which do not change! The old can at least pray for those who hold the reins, that they may be rightly guided.

It is well to be concerned for those who are where Christ has not been named; I suppose every worthwhile work begins with someone having a vision of what may seem impossible. Sometimes the vision tarries, God has HIS time, and bids His servant wait for the fulfillment, it will surely come (Habakkuk 2 vs 3, "For the vision is yet for the appointed time; It hastens toward the goal and it will not fail. Though it tarries, wait for it; For it will certainly come, it will not delay.").

We had rain during the night, almost the first since Christmas, so Blyth and Jan have had almost unbroken sunshine for their time at the beach. They are due home in a couple of days and I expect they will be glad to come, temperature has fallen at least ten degrees and it is cool and windy to-day.

Much love to you all from
Dad

P.O. Box 650
Kabul, Afghanistan
February 26th 1974

Dearest Dad

Today is another memorable day! I must say somewhat unexpected, but we have another exit visa! It almost seems to be an annual event now.

As you know we have been working along under no contract and it did seem that things were going very slowly indeed with progress towards making a new one. However, today I received a call to go over to the visa office and was told that instead of a residence visa we were being given an exit visa. This may take effect in fifteen days from now but I am seeking an extension until the end of May. I feel it would be good for the children to finish the school year properly as they are all doing fairly well this year. I would also like to finish the ophthalmology text book I have been working on. It cannot be rushed of course, writing it takes time and thought and there are also illustrations and translations to think of as well.

I am sorry for Monika, as she faces yet another disruption. This time I will be able to do much more in packing up.

Love, Howard

*A Koochi camel train, they can travel up to
1000 km in a year.*

P.O. Box 650
Kabul, Afghanistan
March 17ᵗʰ 1974

Dearest Dad

Here we are like birds in the wilderness again! Our house is stripped and empty and we are just about to take off once more.

It all came to a head yesterday. I had been trying for almost two weeks to get the Foreign Ministry to agree to give me a one month re-entry visa so that I could leave the country and make arrangements for the family and allow the girls to finish out their year at

273

school here in Kabul. My last hope was the British Ambassador who had very gamely asked for an extension. To my surprise they turned him down.

We had hoped that we would be able to sell the car here and leave in peace by plane, but this did not happen as we were only given a three day exit visa and this meant that there was no time to sell the car. Thus we are setting off this morning after breakfast.

The truck with our household goods is going in front of us and we will meet it in Herat in order to cross the border to Mashad. There we have been able to contact the Medical School and they are willing to store our things until we can get back in September (if this seems the right thing to do). Dr. Hanton is getting a place for us in UK until May in order to allow the girls to finish off their school year.

I will keep in touch as we drive along, we will spend a little time with the Wilsons in Teheran and then see Monika's sister in Germany. I hope we will arrive in UK before the end of the first week in April.

Well, this is the end of an exciting and worthwhile eight years. Looking back much has been accomplished, but how much remains still to be done!

Thanks and praise to Him!

Love to all
Howard and Monika

Teheran, Iran
April 2nd 1974

Dearest Dad

I'm glad I waited on here, for yesterday was one of those pivotal days in one's life.

Quite unexpectedly I was able to get an interview with the Chancellor of Mashad in his Teheran office. Our talk lasted about forty five minutes and covered all the work and contract in detail. He agreed to most of what I had asked. There is a large leprosarium in Mashad and he agreed that I could continue the plastic surgery work I had been doing part time in Afghanistan. The University would pay half the cost of our house rent and a salary. The only difficulty he raised was that of getting permission from the various government departments for my coming. I think he was keen for me to come. This will take about two months to get, so we will not know for sure for two months what we are going to do. He will write to London about it.

I have been thinking about our trip back to UK and talking it over with Monika. We have a feeling that it would be good to visit the relations of Monika in Poland and East Germany as we go back to UK. It means a slight deviation from our normal route but I think it would be worth it. I expect we will be back in the UK by the 25th when the house in Pettit's Lane will be available. We would like the children to finish off their school year there and as soon as that is finished we will come down to NZ by way of the States. I think we would take the return excursion ticket which allows us to get off in Teheran on the way back.

As it is, we hope to push on towards Tabriz tomorrow, then through Turkey, Bulgaria and up through Romania, Hungary, Czechoslovakia and into Poland, across the southern part of East

Germany to Frankfurt, up to Varel to see foster mother, and then across the channel from Germany or Holland. I think we will all be glad to get to UK!

Fondest love from us all
Howard

> 260 Pettit's Lane North
> Romford, England
> May 8th 1974

Dearest Dad

Well, at last! You must think that Howard dropped me off somewhere along the way. Thank you for writing so faithfully and of course your prayers which we were aware of all along the way.

It was a trip I had not looked forward to very much, however it turned out to be very good and unique. I am always a nervous bundle on journeys, whether or not there is traffic on the road.

Howard was a good balance in this matter and only got impatient a couple of times. The girls too were the best travelling companions one could wish for. The car behaved very well and we didn't have even one puncture.

The highlights for me were to visit the old countries from which I came, and to meet up with Auntie Maria and my five cousins. I only was sorry that I had no Polish and German bibles with me, but someone here will help me get some to them. They keep up the old religion without knowing anything from the Word. Bytom is a black and dirty industrial area and a couple of my relations work in the mines. They all have to work, life is tough, but they seem cheerful and relaxed.

We went on to see the place where I was born and although I did not recognize the house, Howard took a photo of the church where my mother went to daily. It had a great mission interest. Howard felt like staying overnight but I wanted to get away, it was still a military base and reminded me too much of 1945. We drove seven hours without stopping for lunch and got to Gorlitz, where we crossed into the D.D.R. Despite the fact we got there at 5 pm we had to cross right through East Germany on one of the three transit routes. We just went off the road a little to drive from Hernnhut to Rennersdorf, where I lived on the farm as a refugee for five years. Here I recognized every house and things had hardly changed. I asked if my foster father from the farm was still alive, an old ladies eyes lit up as she recognized me, I could only send greetings up the hill where I had spent five wonderful years.

We had to press on because of time and also a strange car in a village would soon come to the notice of the police. It was all very exciting to me. We crossed the border into West Germany at midnight –all out of the car! – just in case we had extra passengers, I guess.

Foster mother was her old self but physically weaker. We contributed to a new hearing aid which she badly needs, without it she is stone deaf.

I really enjoyed the tulip fields in Holland and our visit of Floyd's work amongst the Hippies on the house boats in Amsterdam.

I turned down three meetings and a missionary conference, I suppose I am stunned from all the happenings over the past year and felt I had no word from the Lord.

Much love, we are all well,
Monika

P.S. I'll have to take some meetings here, promised four places for a little later. In NZ I might take none. I don't like going over things which are now in the past, maybe I'll feel different later on.

Monika with her foster mother, en route to England.

260 Pettit's Lane North
Romford, England
June 23rd 1974

Dearest Dad

The main feature of the past week has been a quickening of momentum, the pace has quickened until I seem to be running now just to keep up.

We felt that the Lord would show us what to do during the last week. We had been praying about several things, first Mashad. As I looked into this, we felt that we needed a visa. I phoned the Iranian Consul to find out if any letter had arrived from Iran, but was told that if I had a job in Mashad then I should go to Iran on a tourist visa for three months and during that time a visa would be issued from Teheran. He told me this was the way all visas were in practice obtained, as the bureaucracy in Teheran could never produce visas in time to send to overseas embassies.

The second was regarding Monika's health, this is perhaps more important, as you know that she has not been so well the past months after returning to Kabul. We saw the doctor who had seen her in 1966. He spent a good hour going over her and taking a full history again. At the end of it he said that she was in excellent health and that we should not allow this to be a factor in preventing us from going overseas once more. New X-rays will be taken this coming week and I am to have a final session with him after that.

Thus it did seem as if we should return to Iran as planned, regardless of whether we hear back again from Mashad or not.

I wonder if when we come, Monika and I and Joy could stay with you, and Naomi and Faith could stay with Grandma. What do you think? It would be about six weeks and I would be away for about three of the six I think. Could you look over the gifts and correspondence and list the areas in NZ who have supported us in the past couple of years so that I can try to cover each one of them? Thanks very much.

Very much love, yours
Howard

P.O. Box 684
Mashad, Iran
September 15ᵗʰ 1974

Dearest Dad

This will be the first direct news you will have from us here. It is a warm Sunday afternoon and as I sit, I am looking out on the golden dome of the Shrine of Mashad. The temperature is just delightful, with lovely warm days and cool nights.

Just to go back to Auckland, which is still less than a week away (it seems ages to us!!!) I thank the Lord for His goodness to us in the leave taking. He spared the sadness which would come naturally for us both at the parting, which in human terms could be the last. I had thought that we might be able to help you more as you grew older, and still hope that you might come and spend time in Mashad. However it still seems to be the other way around, we are still receiving and not giving as we hoped. I would have wished for some quiet days together at the end, as we had in Napier before the ship sailed. You and Mum stood out in our memories of this time at home, and I am especially thankful that the girls had a chance to get to know you and appreciate you. Mum has changed, mellowed and her extraordinary generosity surprised me.

When we arrived in Mashad the Professor of Ophthalmology was there to meet us with his first assistant and the boys with the Range Rover. They had completed the long journey from UK without further trouble. They drove us to a small hotel near the Shrine where we are still at the moment. There is no doubt they expect us and are ready for us and are paying the bill at the Hotel.

So far we have had a rather depressing tramp around houses for rent. Prices are high. They took the Range Rover into the Customs House and want to charge about $2000 customs duty for it. Hope we can find a house soon and get down to work.

Fondest love from us all
Howard

P.O. Box 684
Mashad, Iran
October 16ᵗʰ 1974

Dearest Dad

I trust spring has fully come by now and that you are well. It is hard to imagine that we have been here a month. The days don't have enough hours in them at present. What a frustrating place this can be at times.

Things in the house are taking shape now. Today we are having hot water for the first time, and Howard is soaking in the bath right now. We have had workmen in nearly every day, or waited in vain all day for them to turn up.

Money just disappears, I spend $3 on a pound of meat a day alone. They just cut you any old piece and you can either mince it or stew it. So far that's all we have been able to do on our picnic cooker. We bought a gas stove and had it connected but the fellow put the piece for the oven in upside down and also broke the thermostat. So we had to contact the dealer, who has come but he has not brought the right piece so far. The glass is finally in all the windows and the curtain railings are up.

Today our telephone was cut off, possibly because the company who had rented this house has outstanding bills. Well, all these interruptions occur when the girls and I are conducting school. They are on the third set now and we have nearly caught up with NZ. They are doing their lessons all right, Naomi is responding best of all, Faith gets frustrated and Joy will not settle down to work unless I am sitting beside her. The girls are quite lonely here but not too bad. The yard is long and has a paved path all around it, so they take turns on Naomi's bike or the roller skates for daily exercise.

Usually we walk together to the shops which are nearby but across a busy road. I wish I had a tin of pineapple or marmite or peanut butter or a packet of soup and so on. We can do without these things, though we have only had fruit every day for pudding.

On Monday night 5 or 6 women, mainly foreigners married to Iranians come together for a tea party in alternate homes. It's for the sake of the children, to keep up their English. There are around 16 children and they have a good time.

It is Ei'd, the end of the fast, we have been invited out quite a lot. We are over the worst here. Space is gone. Much love, Monika

8 Currie Avenue
Hillsborough, Auckland
November 15ᵗʰ 1974

My dear Monika

Even if your letter of October 16ᵗʰ did take almost four weeks to make the three day journey to New Zealand, how thankful I was to have it and to know something of the 'growing pains' of getting settled into the new surroundings! How very frustrating that the man made mistakes in the installation of the gas stove.

I can more easily imagine what it has meant for you to have to cook on a picnic stove day after day. When I was about ten years old we were so poor the only cooking appliance my mother had was a small, two-burner, kerosene cooker, and for two or three years all the meals were prepared on that until they were able to buy a grate that burnt wood and coal. For bathing and washing, water was heated in a four gallon kerosene tin over an open fire in the yard; for the bath we used a large oval tub. It will be the anniversary of mother's birthday in a couple of days – Sunday November 17th 1855 – one hundred and nineteen years ago!

I am so glad that the girls have each been able to settle down to study and have caught up so quickly with the NZ pupils. I did not realize that you would be posting the school lessons to and from regularly and hope there is not a long delay in lessons that occurs with letters. If only there was a good mail service, how gladly we would send a little variety in food! It will be a case of when you live in Iran, you eat Iranian food.

No more just now
God bless you all!
Much love, from Dad

Chapter 15
The Parting

Dad, age 82.

8 Currie Avenue
Hillsborough Auckland
February 7th 1976

My dearest Howard and Monika

I didn't mean to grizzle about the long gap in letters, I thought it may be from the local post office conditions again. In any case I don't want to become a drag, for twenty two years you have written almost every week and I have twenty two manila files containing your correspondence!

Sunday 8th – this afternoon I accompanied Blyth & Jan across to Mother's for an afternoon tea to celebrate her birthday. I think it was more than a coincidence that her brother Neil and Gwen had been there yesterday. It turns out that Gwen has recently had the same treatment that is proposed for my shortness of breath. I thought it was time to see Dr. Wilson about it, so went along last week. He sent me to a radiologist for a chest X-ray and he reported the left lung cavity had an accumulation of fluid. The doctor arranged for me to go in a few days to Greenlane Hospital where the specialist will decide what to do.

Mother's new place is pretty well in order now, and looks quite nice, except that she has the shower-cubicle filled with cartons of junk. All the cupboards are full to over flowing, the "opportunity" shops run by the various churches are too tempting. She was wearing a smart pair of colored shoes that cost 30 cents, had a dress to match that cost a dollar and a hat to complete the outfit for 35 cents!

Much love from
Dad

Mother.

PO Box 684
Mashad, Iran
22nd Feb. 1976

Dearest Dad

I was certainly surprised to hear about your pleural effusion, though looking back there is no doubt you had it for some time, and that this has been mainly responsible for your breathlessness and feeling of lassitude in recent months. I have not heard further from you or Blyth since you went over to Mum's place so guess that you must by now have been in and out of Greenlane. I hope this gets to you at Currie Ave! I suspect that last year you had pleurisy and pneumonia which did not clear up completely and left behind the pleural effusion.

Looking ahead to the summer, I still have not heard back from John Salmon about the possibility of doing his locum in Tunbridge Wells, but even if offered I would not feel free to go there unless you were fit enough to join us. Otherwise, we would come straight home on June 15th and spend as much time in New Zealand as possible.

Suffice it to say that our ties here, as mentioned last week, are much lighter and it would not be difficult for us to relocate at the end of our present contract. Weather has been cold again and Monika and I have had sore throats and head colds for the past couple of days.

With much love from us all,
We have been thinking much of you.
Howard

Howard with leprosy patient.

8 Currie Avenue
Hillsborough Auckland
February 27th 1976

My dearest Howard and Monika

How quickly the days slip by! I waited until my visit to the outpatients department at Greenlane today, before commencing this, so that you could have up-to-date news. Since the aspiration of fluid a fortnight ago breathing has been much easier. This morning they took an X-ray and the consultant was surprised that there appeared to be no fresh accumulation of fluid. In conversation he told me that according to the usual expectation of life tables published by the Insurance companies, at 81 it would be six months, so there are many who exceed the tables.

I also asked him about continuing to live alone, and he strongly advised getting on the waiting list of some comfortable home, as I will feel less and less like housekeeping.

I also did not wish to leave affairs between Mother and me unsettled, so went across to her place early this week, told her the present position and its possible outcome and said I had come so that if she felt I had wronged her in any way, I might be able to put things right. For the next hour I heard all the stories you have so often heard, and some I hadn't heard before, without contradiction from me. When she had said what she wanted, I said I had not come to answer charges or vindicate myself; if all that she said was true, I am sorry she has had such a dreadful husband, and I could only ask her to forgive. We cannot live life over again nor recall the past, I am just what I have always been, and I am not likely to change, but at least we may be at peace with one another.

Well, you may guess how glad she was to have it clear that she had always been right and waited for me to say so! So I am forgiven.

At least it means, that when I depart she will have no regrets that I had never put things right. Since then, Blyth has told her that if she has truly forgiven, she will not continue to bring up the past.

We are having some nice autumn weather, after a summer that never began; Thursday morning the temperature was down to 9.9C, the coldest February morning since 1931!

Much love to you all from
Dad

PO Box 684
Mashad Iran
March 14th 1976

Dearest Dad

No need to tell you that we are constantly remembering you to the Lord and that we love you all very much. With every letter we try to imagine your situation and your feelings toward them.

I know how you feel about hospitals, doctors and all these modern tests, because I like to stay clear of these things myself and find them very upsetting. Yet, the Lord's grace and strength are also sufficient for those things and the opportunities for witness wonderful.

We are so glad that you have felt some benefit since the fluid is gone.

Howard needs to know from the Lord whether or not to call overseas work to a halt and return home for the children's sake and also so that he can get a position somewhere. Or should we continue as we are here, or any place, not taking the children home until they completed their schooling by correspondence? Oh, it is hard to know what to do for the best! I think that Howard would not be happy in any home country for long, although he says he is ready for any change. We wonder if we are needed here.

Well dear Dad, I know you are praying with us.

Very much love from us all
Monika

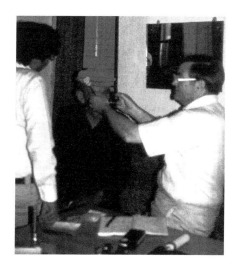

Howard fitting a patient with glasses.

8 Currie Ave
Hillsborough Auckland,
March 29th 1976

My dearest Howard & Monika

Your letter of March 9th has just arrived, almost three weeks on the way, so I have telegrammed you to accept John Salmon's offer of the locum. A reply letter from me would not reach you for another fortnight and the poor chap has already been waiting so long for your reply!

Maybe what is in the back of my mind could be the hope that, for the sake of the girls, you would not wait too long before coming off the field to take a position or set up private practice. It seems to me that Britain would offer far more scope for all of you than would NZ. I am not trying to sway your decision in such a matter, it is one in which you should both be waiting on the Lord and in which you should be clearly guided and agreed. It does matter to Him where we live.

It is quite possible that your diagnosis of the fluid being a legacy from earlier attacks of pleurisy is correct. I have not dismissed the likelihood of it being a primary carcinoma. With Dave and Ted both in my mind, I have long thought my end may come the same way. However, when the tentative diagnosis of a lung tumor was made, immediately the Lord gave me peace about it, and I have no dread on that score. If your diagnosis proved correct that would be His business, but I am not building on that. At 81 the sands of time are running out and something else would crop up.

Now I must run, I want to visit a patient in hospital.

Much love to you all from
Dad

8 Currie Ave
Hillsborough Auckland
June 5th 1976

My dearest Howard and Monika

First of all welcome once again to England, which with all its failure and decay, is "This England" still. I am so glad that you had such a comparatively short-lasting journey and hope all went well, with a comfortable trip to Tunbridge Wells.

I went to the Outpatient Clinic at Greenlane Hospital on May 26th, a day earlier than my appointment, as I was getting desperate for relief. I took a packed bag with me and was admitted to a single room at once. Within two hours they had aspirated two litres of fluid and inserted a drainage tube which drew off another litre by gravity within 24 hrs. Drainage by vacuum pump followed for several days with three insufflations of Atebrin powder. No need to pursue details to a doctor! The outcome is; no left lung, no cure, a face that now looks ten years older, and a very weary old man.

So thankful that Ken and Kay took me in on discharge for a few days and they are so attentive; heater, electric blanket etc. as the weather feels chilly to me.

I am ever so thankful to know you will occupy a Compton missionary cottage while here.

June 7th – I have been just too weary to finish this…am not picking up strength as expected and will be glad to accept Ken and Kay's offer to keep me here a few days longer…

Much love to you all from
Dad

Balliol College, Oxford
England
14th July 1976

Dearest Dad

Well, what a surprise! We never thought to see you in Edenvale Home! I am sure this is the best thing at this time, and we are glad you got a place so quickly. It will give us a chance to help you pack up Currie Avenue when we come.

We are booked to fly on Air India on Sunday 20th of July, the day I officially finish my locum at Tunbridge Wells. We will take off about 7:15 pm and fly direct to Bombay. We change there and fly to Sydney, with several stops on route. We arrive in Auckland at 3:30pm Tuesday afternoon. Please do not come out in the cold to meet us, I am sure Blyth could do that, or we could get a taxi.

I will have the chance at this eye congress I am attending here in Oxford to see many different people. I might get some idea regarding future plans. It does seem a good time to apply for a job in England, but Monika and I still have no clear guidance to stay here.

Love and greetings to all at number 42. Could you please confirm with the Comptons and Fred Swallow.

Love from us all
Howard

Last visit to Dad, July 1976.

In flight from Bombay/Teheran
2ⁿᵈ September 1976

Dearest Dad

Well here we are again! We all thought much of you as the plane winged its way from Auckland. I find that expression of my thoughts at moments of emotion, a difficulty. This time was no exception. I suppose, humanly speaking, the chances of seeing each other again are slight. My deliberate policy of spending the great bulk of time in Asia has meant that we have not seen much of each other for many years! Well, one day we will make up for lost time. I appreciate your genuine desire to keep me at the work the Lord has called me to, and I am grateful beyond words for your friendship and love over the years.

Of course I had wished to play a more active role in helping you during your days of illness, and can only pray that the Lord will graciously shorten the pain you are at present suffering. I certainly could not have wished this for you!

We have arrived, but not without difficulty and even danger! At Bombay the pilot, an elderly man, made a mistake when landing. He brought the plane in to land far too fast and we hit the ground hard. The airport buildings flashed past and the far end of the runway rapidly came in sight. He jammed on the brakes and the 747 began to swerve off the runway and slithered to a halt, a shout away from the barriers at the end of the runway. Faith looked out the window and saw one of the two engines burst into flame. A few seconds later the same engine on the opposite wing caught fire. The cabin-staff were undecided whether to get the passengers off or not. Eventually they asked them to sit down and a few minutes later a foam truck came out and began to spray foam on the two engines. All the passengers were taken off, and we waded through the foam onto the buses. We went to the terminal and waited for more than an hour for the bags to come off.

We spent a night in the Harigan Hotel, on a beach near the airport. Now we are on Air France, also overcrowded, but we were determined to get on. One day late we will, D.V., arrive in Mashad. Psalm 103 has been ringing in my ears, over this time!

Much love from us all,
We are all well.
Howard

Greenlane Hospital
Nov. 26th 1976

My dearest Howard and Monika

The sharp chest pains I had back when you were here have gradually phased down, and instead given place to aching bone and tissue pain in back and lumbar region, which does not respond much to the elixir methadone and largactol, I am receiving p.r.n. I have just had a kind discussion with the house surgeon, who has promised to add to my night schedule to ease my night pain, "to repeat as required".

You will understand my plea for the mercy of God, that He will call me quickly.

Looking back over the long years they have been filled with His love and goodness, and gratitude for your own part in your own love to me.

Till we meet in the morning.

His blessing with you all – it is too late for more.

All my love to my children, from
Dad

PO Box 684
Mashad Iran
Dec. 25th 1976

Dearest Dad

Well, today I thought it just possible I might be on my way to you, but it became clear over the last couple of days that this was not to be. I sent my tickets off to British Airways in high hopes, as it seemed they would accept the five tickets we had for London as a credit for a ticket to Auckland. However, having seen the tickets they could only offer a trip to London and then once more I would have to buy a cheap excursion ticket to Auckland. I reluctantly gave up the idea, which appealed to my restless nature, but basically was an expression of heart love to you, and desire to be with you during your time of deep distress and suffering. We have cancelled all appearances at parties or festivities during this season, and are just going to the English service, conducted by Dr. Thomas, this afternoon. My heart has felt little like festivities. Please forgive me that at your hour of deepest need I could not be there to help.

Christmas has come with very cold weather, for two or three days the sky has been cloudy and snow has fallen. We all opened presents this morning under the large and beautiful Christmas tree.

Nothing seems clear at the hospital any longer. Recently I was approached by a local ophthalmologist who has opened a 100 bed private eye clinic here, wanting me to help him after hours or full time. The money was of course more, but I explained to him that this is not what I was here for. Life would become very complicated if I began to compete for rich patients with the local ophthalmologists. It seems to me that the Hospital and University are trying hard to push me into some such work. Basically I think this is a narrow minded reaction to the fact that I was given the title of Professor and Head of Eye department when I first came. The other alternative being that I take out Iranian citizenship. Otherwise in the changed climate that prevails, there is little future for us here. We are ready to stay or go, and trust Him completely to do what is right. The pendulum is swinging against foreigners now.

However these are small worries really, though we are not keen on uprooting once more.

Much love from us all, in Him
Howard

Stan Harper went home to be with the Lord he loved, on December 27ᵗʰ 1976. At his specific request, there was no public service at the time of his passing, and just a small group of some closest to him buried his mortal remains at Waihi Lawn Cemetery.

"With Christ which is far better."

299

Epilogue – "Central Asia Awakes"

Dad's heart has always been in Central Asia, and even after we returned to England from the mission field in Iran, he migrated back home to Central Asia whenever possible. Most summer holidays he would get together a small medical team and travel from England to Pakistan for a fortnight of intensive eye camp work. As a teenager I joined my parents on several eye camps in the sparsely populated areas of the Karakoram mountain range in northern Pakistan. In February of 1991 Dad was able to purchase land there, near the Gilgit River, and construct a permanent Eye Clinic, which still serves the many tribal mountain people of Northern Pakistan.

During our time in Tunbridge Wells, Kent, my parents developed close links with Ron and Nan George, a family who, like us, had returned from missionary service. Ron started People International, a ministry to countries that were closed to the gospel, like those of Central Asia. In the early eighties the only way to enter these countries was on a two week tourist visa and Dad and Ron joined an organized tour, entering Uzbekistan and Tajikistan for the first time as a tourist. Their visit happened to coincide with an International Book Fair and they were able to bring in bible portions in Tajik and Uzbek. Throughout the visit there was close surveillance by KGB agents who beat up one of the members of the group on the way to the theatre.

In Bukhara, Uzbekistan, they attended the small Baptist church. During the meeting a few elderly Russian women and men prayed fervently, but Dad's eye was on a younger Uzbek man present in the congregation. At the end of the service the KGB agents assigned to the tour group, spread amongst the members and tried to prevent them meeting the tourists. Dad was able to snatch a hurried conversation with the young Uzbek believer who had come to faith whilst studying in Latvia.

"How can we help you?" asked my Dad.

"Bring me one thousand New Testaments in Uzbek," Replied the young man.

"What will you do with them?"

"I have fifty people interested in becoming believers." He said.

"Only the book of John has been translated into Uzbek," Dad offered, "I'll bring them for you next year, I promise."

The following year Dad returned to Uzbekistan on another tour and smuggled in a bag of John's gospels. The church in Bukhara was closed and the KGB hounded every step of the tour group. They were able to leave copies of John's gospel in different places, but not with the earnest young man who had requested them. Later Dad discovered he had been arrested during the course of the year, imprisoned and put in a psychiatric ward. During a temporary release he was killed by KGB agents.

A decade later, the doors to Central Asia were flung open in an unexpected way. My husband Jonathan and I, were with my parents in a small hotel in Strasburg, on our way back from a ski trip. Dad flicked on the TV to catch the news. A video footage of the execution of communist dictator, Nicolai Ceausescu and his wife Elena, was being shown, displaying their dead bodies pocked with bullets. More staggering to me than the monumental event being replayed on all the TV channels, was the "unholy" excitement of my Dad.

"Today is the beginning of the collapse of the communist empire. Soon the doors of Central Asia will be open to the gospel, "announced Dad, "I've waited forty five years for this!"

Dad was fifteen when he first promised God he would go for Him to Central Asia. He was now sixty years old.

Dad was right, for after the fall of Ceausescu the communist regime rapidly disintegrated, and by 1991 it was on its knees. While many of the Central Asian countries eagerly declared independence from Russia, their new found autonomy plunged their healthcare systems into crisis as financial and medical support from Russia was severed. By the end of 1991 Dad had negotiated four agreements to set up eye- care programs with the governments of Uzbekistan, Tajikistan, Mongolia and Kirghizstan. At the age of 61 he embarked on the very real challenge of establishing eye-care centers in these different countries.

In 1995 an eye clinic was opened in Tashkent, Uzbekistan, but it was requisitioned by the government a year later. Humanitarian aid was given to war-stricken Tajikistan, although establishment of an eye clinic was not realized. An eye centre was opened in Ulan Bator, Mongolia in 1997, but within a short period of time it was closed by the government who claimed its premises. Three agreements, however, out of the four, were utilized to bring some measure of help and Christian witness to these countries.

After 9/11, American military control of Afghanistan allowed Dad to return "home". He found the former NOOR Eye Clinic desolate. It had become the domain of roaming camels and was stripped of everything of value, including the electric wires and plumbing. Dad went to the Minister of Health and asked to rebuild the clinic. It was rebuilt and reopened as a general hospital in 2004.

"Has it been worth it Dad?" I asked recently. "What have you gained from all your efforts in Central Asia?"

"I'm in it for the gold…" he twinkled, "disciples of Jesus. Maybe now there are a few more nuggets here and there."

Israel, summer 2008. The supper dishes have been cleared and again it is story time with Dad. Tonight there will be a family premiere of a musical Dad has compiled: "Central Asia Awakes". We were surprised by his latest development in, not only medical, but musical interest. He has written the script and someone else wrote the songs. Jonathan and I, our three boys, and Mum and Dad, all gather in the sitting room.

"Dad, you can be the narrator." I hand him a photocopied part. "I think we are going to have to read the words of the songs as none of us can sight read music."

"Jonathan, would you like to be the Afghan King? We'll do without props tonight. Imagine a room in the Kabul palace where you are pacing back and forth saying, "Never! Never will I allow Christians into my country!""

"But I want to be the Afghan King," John, our youngest son, pipes up.

"Why don't you be the young Uzbek man? He gets killed for being a Christian." I suggest.

We take turns in reading our parts and the songs. The heat of the day lingers, and wafts in waves through the open sliding doors into the sitting room.

"When will Central Asia be reached with the gospel? When will it be the turn of Central Asia to see the light?" My dad's forehead beads with sweat as he reads.

As the first performance of "Central Asia Awakes" draws to a close I am glad our boys could share a glimpse of the calling that has steered Dad and Mum to take their unorthodox and often lonely paths. The musical has been piercing in its devotion. I swallow back tears as I listen to a love story, my own father's love story with God and Central Asia. In the background I hear the strains of another story, my Granddad's love for his son, sent far away to Central Asia to show the Father's love.

Israel
August 9th 2010

Dear Reader

My prayer and hope is that there will be some among you who will take up the torch for Central Asia.

Mum and Dad continue to invest their lives in Afghanistan. Dad says: "Currently our UK based Charity, Vision International, is involved in finishing an Eye Clinic in Kabul and the running of a School that offers a parallel English and Afghan curriculum to both boys and girls.

"Monika has been involved in establishing the English department of the school and training teachers. It is a thriving school teaching mainly the Hazara minority group in Afghanistan. We have reached 6th Grade at our school and plan to develop a curriculum that will provide a complete secondary education at international level. We urgently need to build a new school, as currently we are renting premises and our school is full to overflowing!"

My parents hope to celebrate their 50th wedding anniversary this month. Again, I am overwhelmed by God's grace to us as a family – His grace has won us and overcome us.

Yours faithfully
Faith (Harper) Goldberg

P.S. If you would like to make a donation to the work of Vision International, please contact me at fg@generalmail.com or postal address: P.O. Box 179, Kiriat Tivon 36000, Israel.

Howard and Monika enjoy their
Jubilee Year together, 2010.